Tea and Health

Science Behind the Myths

Tea and Health

Science Behind the Myths

N. Ghosh Hajra

UBSPD
UBS Publishers' Distributors Pvt. Ltd.
New Delhi • Bangalore • Kolkata • Chennai • Patna • Bhopal
Ernakulam • Mumbai • Lucknow • Pune • Hyderabad

UBS PUBLISHERS' DISTRIBUTORS PVT. LTD.

5 Ansari Road, **New Delhi**-110 002
Phones: 011-23273601-4, 23266645-47 • Fax: 23276593, 23274261
E-mail: ubspd@ubspd.com

10 First Main Road, Gandhi Nagar, **Bangalore**-560 009
Phones: 080-22253903, 22263901, 22263902, 22255153 • Fax: 22263904
E-mail: ubspdbng@dataone.in

8/1-B Chowringhee Lane, **Kolkata**-700 016
Phones: 033-22521821, 22522910, 22529473 • Fax: 22523027
E-mail: ubspdcal@cal.vsnl.net.in

60 Nelson Manickam Road, Aminjikarai, **Chennai**-600 029
Phones: 044-23746222, 23746351-2 • Fax: 23746287
E-mail: ubspd@che.ubspd.com

Ground Floor, Western Side, Annaporna Complex, Naya Tola,
Patna-800 004 • Phones: 0612-2672856, 2673973, 2686170
Fax: 2686169 • E-mail: ubspdpat1@sancharnet.in

143, M.P. Nagar, Zone-I, **Bhopal**-462 011
Phones: 0755-4203183, 4203193, 2555228 • Fax: 2555285
E-mail: ubspdbhp@sancharnet.in

No. 40/7940-41, Kollemparambil Chambers, Convent Road,
Ernakulam-682 035 • Phones: 0484-2353901, 2363905 • Fax: 2365511
E-mail: ubspdekm@dataone.in

2nd Floor, Apeejay Chambers, 5 Wallace Street, Fort,
Mumbai-400 001 • Phones: 022-56376922, 56376923, 56028017
Fax: 56376921 • E-mail: ubspdmum@mum.ubspd.com

1st Floor, Halwasiya Court Annexe, 11MG Marg, Hazaratganj,
Lucknow-226 001 • Phones: 0522-2294134, 2611128
Fax: 2294133 • E-mail: ubspdlko@lko.ubspd.com

680 Budhwar Peth, 2nd floor, Near Appa Balwant Chowk, **Pune**-411 002
Phone: 020-24433976 • Fax: 020-56028921
E-mail: ubspdpune@rediffmail.com

NVK Towers, 2nd floor, 3-6-272/B, Himayat Nagar,
Hyderabad-500 029 • Phones: 040-23262572, 23262573, 23262574
Fax: 040-23262572 • E-mail: ubspdhyd@vsnl.net

Visit us at www.ubspd.com & www.gobookshopping.com

First Published 2006

Cover Design: Admire Works Design

Printed at: Rajkamal Electric Press, Delhi

To
my wife
who has been a source of inspiration
behind all my activities

Contents

Foreword

Tea is a pleasant, inexpensive, versatile, safe, virtually calorie and sodium free beverage that is enjoyed by people across the globe. It is also a dietary source of biologically active compounds that help prevent a wide variety of diseases. In today's stressful world, tea can play a vital role in improving the quality of human health, especially since consumers in developed countries are becoming more and more health conscious. Scientific progress in the field of tea and health too has been remarkable in the past two decades. Research shows that tea has anti-bacterial, anti-viral, anti-cariogenic and anti-carcinogenic properties. Recent studies also show that polyphenols in tea can lower the risk of cardio-vascular disease. In fact, black and green teas have attributes that can lower the risk of several chronic diseases.

The book *Tea and Health—Science Behind the Myths* offers a timely and comprehensive review of the major health benefits of tea consumption including the anti-oxidative action of tea catechins and polyphenols, and will increase the appreciation of tea as a health drink.

To conclude, I extend my appreciation as well as congratulate Dr. N. Ghosh Hajra for his sincere effort, despite his other engagements, in writing this treatise on tea and health.

I wish him continued success.

N. K. Das, IAS
Chairman, Tea Board of India
Kolkata

Preface

Tea is the most consumed drink in the world after water. It is a refreshing, thirst-quenching natural product that is virtually calorie-free when had without milk and sugar. The role of tea in the promotion of health has been recorded in numerous scientific publications, reviews and presentations at international symposiums and conferences. However, more comprehensive and in-depth studies are needed to thoroughly evaluate the effect of tea drinking on a host of diseases. Further exploration at the cellular level will allow a better understanding of the underlying mechanisms regulating functions in the normal and pathologic states. Development of more specific and sensitive methods, with more representative models, along with the development of good predictive biomarkers will give a better understanding of the interaction of tea and the endogenous systems and other exogenous factors. On-going research into the properties and possible benefits of tea are of tremendous importance to the industry too as it struggles to promote tea over other beverages and to establish, once and for all, the veracity of the various health claims related to tea. In fact, there is a compelling body of scientific information which suggests that selecting tea as a beverage can be the most healthy choice which people can make. Tea should be the beverage of choice in hospitals, which might facilitate recovery of the patients. Tea is a great drink for modern lives.

The purpose of this book is to introduce tea-drinkers to this wonderful beverage, and also to gain more understanding on the positive health effects of tea consumption as regards a chemopreventive role against cardiovascular diseases, cancer and several other diseases.

Every effort has been made to ensure the accuracy of the contents of this book. Because of space limitation, many of the earlier publications are not cited, instead, review articles have been given as reference. However, I would be pleased to hear of any errors/loopholes which have escaped my notice and also welcome suggestion(s) for incorporation in the future edition.

Nikhil Ghosh Hajra

Acknowledgements

I wish to express my gratitude to Sri NK Das, *IAS* Chairman, Tea Board and Sri RS Sukla, *IAS* Deputy Chairman, Tea Board and Sri B Banerjee, *IAS* the then Deputy Chairman of Tea Board for providing me the opportunity and inspiration for publication of this book. I am deeply indebted to Prof. John H. Weisburger, Director Emeritus Institute for Cancer Prevention, American Health Foundation and Prof. Jeffrey Blumberg, Associate Director of Jean Mayer USDA Human Nutrition, Research Centre on Aging, Tufts University for their useful comments on some important portion of the text of this book.

I am also indebted to the tea planters, friends in the tea industry the world over for their constant support during the preparation of the book. It is also a special pleasure to acknowledge the encouragement provided by my colleagues of Darjeeling Tea Research and Development Centre, and Prof SN. Roy, IISWBM, Kolkata, Sri D. Chowdhuri, Deputy Director of the Rubber Research Institute of India, Guwahati.

I would like to acknowledge the help taken in writing this book from various publications and say thanks to the authors for their dedicated work.

I feel obliged and extremely thankful to Sri Vivek Ahuja and his team of UBS Publishers' Distributors Ltd., New Delhi for taking endless pain during its preparation, printing and publication.

I am also thankful to Sri Partha Dey of Technoworld, Kurseong for his support at the time of the preparation of the text and formation of this book.

Finally, I am grateful to my parents and Ms Amrapali Roy for their inspiration right from the time when this book was contemplated.

This publication does not necessarily reflect the views of the Tea Board of India and in no way anticipates the Board's policy in this area. Its content is the sole responsibility of the author.

Nikhil Ghosh Hajra

Chapter 1

History of Tea

Introduction

The natural home of the tea plant is considered to be the fan-shaped area included between the Naga, Manipuri and Lushai Hills along the Assam-Burma frontier in the west, through to China, probably as far as the Che-Kiang (Zhejiang) province in the east, and from this line generally south through the hills of Burma and Thailand into Vietnam[1]. A recent study, based on the geological history of eastern Yunan and the distribution of the *Camellia* species in that area, indicated that the long narrow region of Wenshan and Honghe, located between $22^{0}\,40^{\prime}$–$24^{0}\,10^{\prime}$N and $103^{0}\,10^{\prime}$–$105^{0}\,20^{\prime}$E was the centre of origin of the tea plant[2].

The current distribution patterns of different varieties of tea suggest that the probable centre of origin of tea was near the source of the Irrawaddy River and from there it dispersed to south-eastern China, Indonesia and Assam.

Tea-producing Countries

From the main centres of its primary origin in south-east Asia, tea has spread far and wide into tropical and subtropical areas and adopted broad characteristics corresponding to regions of tropical rainforest, tropical Savannah and summer-rain areas. At present, tea is grown in more than 30 countries. The area, productivity and exports of tea of some major countries are given in Table. 1.1.

Spread of Tea in India

Although a consignment of tea seeds is reported to have been brought from China to India by the East India Company as early as 1774, the history of tea in India

Table 1.1
Area, production and exports of major tea-producing countries during 2004

Country	*Area (ha)*	*Production*	*Exports*	*Productivity (kg/ha)*
		(Million kgs)		
Asia				
Bangladesh	51225	56	12	1093
China	1155000	785	280	679
India	511940	820	184	1602
Indonesia	162000	165	96	1018
Japan	50200	85	–	1693
Sri Lanka	188971	309	291	1635
Turkey	76700	145	5	1890
Vietnam	71000	95	60	1338
Africa				
Kenya	132000	325	326	2462
South America				
Argentina	39000	63	66	1615

Source: Tea Board India, Kolkata and F.O.Licht's World Markets Monthly, U.K.

has its origin in 1823. Major Robert Bruce, while visiting India as a member of a trading mission in 1823, discovered tea plants growing wild in some hills near Rangpur (now Sibsagar), the then capital of Assam[3]. Assam was then a Burmese occupation, but in 1824, war broke out with Burma. Robert Bruce died in the same year. His younger brother Charles Alexander Bruce was appointed in 1824 to command a division of Gumboats in upper Assam. During the progress of hostilities with Burma in 1826 he brought certain plants and seeds which were identified as true tea species, *Camellia*. But there is dispute in this regard.

According to Baildon[4], the tea plant of Assam was discovered by a local Assamese nobleman, Dewan Maniram Dutta Barua, who later worked in the Assam Company for sometime. Dewan Maniram might have brought the plant to the notice of Robert Bruce during his visit to Rangpur in 1823. Further, the role of the Sungpho tribe of Assam in bringing the local plant to the notice of the outside world cannot be ignored. It was a Sungpho chief who supplied the seeds and plants to CA Bruce. This clearly shows that the Sungphos were familiar with the tea plant[5].

In 1834, Lord William Bentinck, the then Governor-General of India, appointed the Tea Committee to recommend suitable areas for tea cultivation in India. The Tea Committee reported that the tea plant was indigenous to Assam, especially its upper reaches. The commercial cultivation of tea in commercial plantations was started with local Assam tea. However, from 1836, onwards, the seed from China[6] was used. A detailed history of the growth and development of tea in India has been provided by Ukers[3] and Ghosh Hajra[7].

Legends about Tea's Reviving Properties

Tea was discovered quite accidentally by the Chinese emperor Shen Nung in 2737 B.C. The 'Divine Healer', as the emperor was called routinely, used to boil his drinking water before consuming it, and one day, some leaves from a tree fell into the pot, producing an excellent tasting and fragrant beverage. The emperor, upon drinking the concoction, proclaimed the beverage as 'heaven sent'. Thus tea was discovered.

Another legend has it that a Buddhist monk named Budhidharma, unable to remain awake during a prolonged meditation, cut off his eyelids and flung them to the ground in desperation. His heroic devotion won the favour of the Gods, who instantly turned his eyelids into the first tea plants. Budhidharma managed to stay awake for the next seven years by chewing nothing but tea leaves and tea became forever mystically linked with Buddhism and meditation.

The refreshing properties of tea have been noted for over 4,000 years and can be corroborated by tea drinkers the world over who experience its reviving properties on a daily basis. In fact, a host of myths and legends about tea's health benefits have been touted through the years, with no one seriously contending that tea drinking is bad for health.

Box 1.1

An invoice of eight chests of Assam tea was sent to London in 1838. The consignment was auctioned in London on January 10, 1839. The high prices of tea at once attracted the attention of enterprising businessmen in Calcutta as well as in London. In 1839, the first private-owned tea company, the Assam Company, was formed in London by the Board of Control and Court of Directors of the East India Company. In March 1840, practically all the East India Company's plantations, except those at Chabua, Dinijoy and two other small gardens, were handed over to the Assam Company. In 1852, when the company emerged as the first successful tea company in the world, its performance attracted many others to invest in tea. Later, through the pioneering efforts of local entrepreneurs mostly Assamese, the plantations began to spread and flourish in other parts of the state including Cachar, Tripura and Sylhet (presently in Bangladesh).

A. Campbell, Superintendent of Darjeeling, pioneered the experimental growth of tea in the hills in early 1841 by planting a few seeds from the China stock around his bungalow, now known as Beechwood located at 2134 metres above sea level. The first trial in Darjeeling, done in 1841 with a few seeds grown in the Kumaon plantations from the China stock, was quite successful. However, the actual commencement of the tea industry in Darjeeling is listed in the year 1856–57. After independence, British planters, who owned about 90 per cent of the estates in the Darjeeling hills, started selling their holdings to local entrepreneurs. By mid-1950s, a large number of estates had changed hands. At present, there are around 70 tea estates functioning in the Darjeeling hills, producing 10–11 million kilos of tea every year.

A few tea estates were also set up in 1862 in Ranchi, a plateau region of the Chotanagpur area of Jharkhand (the then Bihar) state. But it didn't turn out successful due to various reasons. After a lapse of 120 years, in 1982, a small tea plantation company, the Sonapur Tea Estate, started tea cultivation with only two hectares of land in Sonapur—Panwara village of Pothia block in Kishanganj district of Bihar. Subsequently, the cultivation spread to the adjoining blocks—Pothia, Thakurganj and Kishanganj, covering nearly 1,500 hectares.

In Himachal Pradesh, the first commercial plantation was established at Holta near Palampur in 1852, at an elevation of 1260 metres above sea level. Thereafter, the tea industry flourished and expanded in the state covering the Kangra district. The Britishers started a number of tea gardens in the mid-1850s. The seeds for planting were largely obtained from China, however, a small quantity of Chinese hybrid seeds and plants also came from the Kumaon hills of Uttaranchal.

In Uttaranchal, tea plantation spread over 8,800 hectares, covered with the flavoury China-hybrid tea. Most of these plantations, except those in the Dehradun valley at an altitude of about 700 metre, were located far and wide between altitudes of 1,500–2,100 metre. Old tea plantations exist in the districts of Pithoragarh, Champawat, Almora, and Nainital in Kumaon, and Chamoli and Rudraoprayag in Garhwal.

Credit for growing tea in the Nilgiri's in 1832 goes to a Dr Christi. In 1834, a few plants grown from the seeds brought from China were again planted in these hills. The earliest record of commercial tea planting in Peermade in Kerala goes back to 1875. The development of the Kanan Devan Hills by James Finlay and Company in 1878 as an exclusive tea growing area is a landmark in the history of tea planting in this part of the country. Soon, tea cultivation caught up in Wynaad and by 1889, it was taken up on a large scale in the district. In the Anamallais (Coimbatore district), tea estates were developed around 1897. Karnataka came onto the tea map, rather recently.

India is the largest producer and consumer of tea. Almost all the teas produced are 'black', although a small quantity of green tea is also produced. The Darjeeling tea is famous for its muscatel flavour. Assam tea is granular, greyish to black in colour. This tea has a strong bright liquor.

Other Major Tea Growing Countries

China

The history of tea cultivation in China can be traced back to 3,000 years ago. The tea plantations in China are located between 94^0 E to 122^0 E longitude, and from 18^0 N to 37^0 N latitude, on elevations up to 2,600 m. But the areas for economic cultivation are concentrated in the region 102^0E eastwards and 32^0N southwards. The tea growing areas have a humid monsoon climate of the east coast type. In the subtropics of China, the climate is not as dry as the general subtropics: it is moist, has a lot of precipitation and high temperatures in summer[8]. The tea-producing areas are distributed in 19 provinces, viz. Anhui, Jiangxi, Zhejiang, Jiangsu, Hunan, Sichuan, Guangxi, Yunnan, Guizhou, Guangdong, Hainan, Hubei, Taiwan, Fujian, Shanxi, Shandong, Gansu, Henan and Tibet. The four major tea producing provinces—Zhejiang, Hunan, Sichuan and Anhui—together account for 60 per cent of the national output.

The tea areas are divided into four parts—the south China tea area, the south-west China tea area, the south of Yangtse River tea area and the north of Yangtse River tea area. China which produces a variety of teas held a pre-eminent position in tea production and export for a long time. According to the processing methods and technologies, Chinese teas are basically divided into six categories, viz. green tea, black tea, oolong tea, white tea, yellow tea and black-black tea. Of these, green tea forms the main bulk and black tea accounts for about 20 per cent of the total production. Oolong tea is a semi-fermented tea made mainly in Fujian, Guangdong and Taiwan provinces. White tea, a light fermented tea is primarily made in the Fujian province. Black-black tea is a post fermented tea consumed mainly by people living in remote border areas of China.

Sri Lanka

Dr N Wallich of the Calcutta Botanical Gardens sent Assam tea seeds to Sri Lanka (the then Ceylon) in December 1839. The seeds were received by the Royal Botanical Gardens at Peradeniya near Kandy. Thereafter, the Government of Sri Lanka received 200 plants in 1841 which were planted in Nuwara Eliya. Two further consignments of plants were received in early 1841 and 1842 from China and Assam, and were planted in Rothschild estate at Udapusselawa and Pennyland estate, Dolasbage respectively. However, planting of tea in Sri Lanka began in a serious way in the 1880s, essentially as a replacement of coffee which was fast dying out because of an attack of the dreaded coffee rust (*Hemileia vastatrix*).

In Sri Lanka, tea is produced under varied ecological regimes, but for easy reference, these are grouped on the basis of elevation into three broad categories, low (below 600 m), medium (between 601 to 1,200 m) and high elevation (above 1200 m) tea areas. Sri Lanka, however, produces only black tea and almost 98 per cent of it is manufactured by the orthodox method. Plucking continues throughout the year. Currently, Sri Lanka is the leading exporter of tea in the world.

Malawi

In 1878, Jonathan Duncan, a gardener at the Church of Scotland Mission in Blantyre, obtained tea seeds from the botanical gardens in Edinburgh but these failed to grow. Later, in 1886, Dr Elmslie brought another batch of seeds from Edinburgh and a few from Kew Gardens. In his second attempt, Duncan got just two bushes which were planted in the grounds of the Mission in Blantyre. One of these bushes became the ancestor of the original tea plantations in Mulanje and vegetatively propagated bushes from this bush are still growing in the Tea Research Foundation. During 1891, Henry Brown procured a few seeds from Duncan. Half of these he planted in his estate (Thornwood) and other half on a neighbouring estate (Lauderdale) owned by John Moir. From 1908 onwards, tea estates were opened in Mulanje (700 m to 1,000 m elevation) and Cholo (900 m to 1,300 m elevation) districts in the south. Initially planting was done with China hybrids but later Assam jats were introduced. Tea cultivation spread to the northern district of Nkhata Bay in 1960. Although Malawi teas are not so well known as speciality teas, their superb colour and brightness lends them admirably to use in the blending of leading British tea brands.

Kenya

Tea was introduced in Kenya in 1903. Production of tea in Kenya was virtually confined to estates until the

1960s. Then came the special Crops Development Authority (set up in 1960) to develop small-holders' tea production. The Kenyan Government established the Kenyan Tea Development Authority (KTDA) in 1964 to develop tea among the small holder and also to extend cultivation to all suitable areas. At present, 66 per cent of the tea area in Kenya is owned by over 2,00,000 individual growers with an average holding of one acre or slightly more than half a hectare. The principal tea growing districts of Kenya are located in the area lying between Mount Kenya and Lake Victoria on either side of the Rift Valley. The tea estates are spread across either side of the equator. The main tea growing districts include Kericho in the west, followed by Nandi, Sotik, and Kissii around Kericho. Planting is done at an elevational range of 1,600 to 2,250 m. Kenya produces only black tea. About 90 per cent is CTC (cut, tear, and curl) manufacture. Between 8–15 per cent is used for local consumption while the rest is exported. Kenyan tea is very bright, colourful (with a reddish coppery tint) and a pleasant brisk flavour.

Japan

Japan is among the major producers and consumers of tea in the world. Its 50,200 hectares of tea fields yield around 85,000 tons of tea every year. Known for its consumption and export of green tea, Japan imports a wide variety of tea from around the world. The Japanese green tea called *o-cha* has numerous varieties due to the different cultivation and processing methods. Sencha, Gyokuro, Matcha, Kamairicha, Bancha Houjicha are some varieties of green tea that Japan grows. The Japanese also use green tea as an ingredient in ready-to-drink teas, soft drinks, ice cream, biscuits and lollies.

Green tea has been recognised for its digestive capabilities as well as its flavour and soothing aroma. *Sencha* is fresh, grassy, refreshing and cooling. It may be bright green or lighter, with the higher quality teas infusing greener colour and tasting more vegetal than the lesser quality teas, which are paler and grassier. *Sencha Honyama* is pale green in colour and has a clean, flowery flavour that makes it specially relaxing and soothing. *Gyokuro* green tea is the best green tea that Japan produces. Known as pearl dew, *gyokuro* has high chlorophyll content and low tannin. Its leaf is dark emerald green in colour. As it is finely processed, it is powdery. Matcha Uji is a special tea used for the famous Japanese tea ceremony called *Cha-no-yu*. Made from the Gyokuro tea plant, its brewing is done in the traditional way. Bancha Houjicha is crisp and nutty-tasting because the leaves are roasted. This tea is light brown and is served with noodles and sushi. Genmaicha is made by mixing green tea with roasted rice and popcorn. This innovation was made during World War II to meet the tea shortage. Today, Genmaicha is a favourite Japanese treat. The origin of the Japanese tea can be attributed to China. Monks who studied in China during the 11th and 12th centuries brought tea to Japan. Today, drinking tea is a ceremony in Japan which has become a part of the Japanese tradition.

Indonesia

The Dutch can be said to have introduced tea in Indonesia in the 18th century. In those days, the island of Java was used as a staging port by the Dutch East India Company for the onward transportation of Chinese tea. By the early 18th century, Dutch settlers were already establishing tea plantations on the island. Production soon followed in Sumatra and later on the island of Sulawesi. World War II, however, saw a decline in tea business that had become a way of life for the Indonesians for the past 200 years. In 1984, Indonesia's tea industry was revived with much effort and investment. Since the establishment of the Indonesian Tea Board, constant improvement has taken place due to the implementation of modern methods of tea production. Today, Indonesia produces 165,000 tons of tea. Indonesian teas differs from other teas in terms of location, soil, and climate of the tea estates. Tea estates are located in the highlands where volcanic soil and tropical climate is predominant. Though the main product of Indonesia is the black tea and about 80 per cent of it is exported, green tea is also produced here. The bulk of Indonesian tea is grown in the island of Java, and though tea is picked all year round, the best quality is obtained during the dry season of August and September from government-owned estates. Black tea, produced currently from tea plants originally imported from Assam, is mostly exported for blending. Indonesian teas are light and flavourful. It is the only country where tea auction is not conducted in English.

Chemical Constituents of Tea

Tea is composed of unique constituents. The presence of caffeine in tea was discovered in 1827 and it was given the name theine at that time. But later it was seen that the structure and the properties of this substance were exactly the same as caffeine that was identified in coffee in 1820. Then the name theine was dropped.

Theanine was discovered by Y. Sakato in 1950, which is unique to tea, is a kind of amino acid constituting more than half the total amount of amino acids in tea. Major catechins in tea are also unique. The presence of Vitamin C was discovered in green tea by

M Miura and M Tsujimura who worked under Professor U Suzuki. Between 1927 and 1935, Tsujimura investigated the astringent property of tea and isolated epicatechin, epicatechin gallate and epigallocatechin. She determined their structural formulas[9]. In 1950, AB Bradfield, A. British scientist, isolated epigallocatechin gallate and determined its structure by the X-ray diffraction method. Later in the 1950s, EAH Roberts clarified the steric complications of individual catechins in Britain by using the techniques of two-dimensional paper chromatography. He is famous for his research on polyphenolic compounds, theaflavins, and thearubigins in black tea. The presence of essential oils in fresh tea leaves was discovered by Mulder more than 150 years ago. Thereafter, Professor Takei and Professor Yamamoto did extensive research on green and Taiwan black tea respectively and identified more than 30 compounds. Their research undoubtedly became the base for future research in the field. Later Professor Tei Yamanishi, successor of Professor Tsujimura, also became renowned for her research on the isolation of aroma compounds by gas chromatography. More than 600 aroma compounds have been identified till today.

Tea Drinking Around the World

Tea is served in a number of different ways in India (Fig. 1.1). It is mostly brewed in water and served with milk and sugar. On railway stations, trains and streetcorners, sweet milky tea is poured from hot kettles into disposable cups or mugs.

Tea is always served to guests in modern Chinese homes as a sign of welcome and hospitality. The Chinese serve a range of different teas which are brewed in glasses, covered mugs or little Chinese teapots and

Fig. 1.1 Tea served at railway station; tea served with lemon
Courtesy: The Heritage of Indian Tea by DK Taknet

bowls. The modern Japanese society has kept alive its famous '*Cha-no-yu*' or tea ceremony from the early days of the Zen Buddhist monks. The tea served in the tea ceremony is called *matcha* (pronounced 'mahcha') and is a powdered tea of the highest quality. *Matcha* is beaten with lukewarm water with a whisk in a small porcelain bowl and served. The Japanese believe that "tea is more than an idealisation of the form of drinking and it is a religion of the art of life". Today, Japanese mostly drink green tea, but there is a noticeable trend towards black tea among certain sections.

In Tibet, green tea is broken up and boiled in water, then strained into a churn and mixed with goat's or yak's milk, salt, and butter.

In Iran and Afghanistan, people drink green tea as a thirst quencher and black tea as a warm refreshment from little porcelain bowls. In Egypt, tea is brewed without milk and served in glasses, and sometimes flavoured with sugar or mint leaves. In Morocco, black tea is brewed with sugar and mint in a long-spouted pot and is then poured in a thin stream into tall glasses.

In Turkey, black tea is served in curved glasses and offered it on trays to visitors throughout the day. Russians drink both black and green teas usually from glasses. They in general take sugar cubes or a spoonful of jam before sipping the tea.

Like the British and the Indians, most of the African people drink strong tea with milk. Tea is also a widely consumed beverage in America. Iced teas comprise about 80 per cent of all teas consumed in the United States. But the fashion of drinking hot black tea with milk is now growing. The 'gourmet' or 'speciality teas' are getting quite popular among elite Americans. A wide variety of speciality shops and mail order companies offer a carefully chosen range of teas from all over the world.

References

1. Harler, CR (1966). *Tea Growing*. Oxford University Press, London. p. 162.
2. Yu, F (1986). Discussion on the originating place and the originating centre of tea plant (in Chinese). *J. Tea Sci.* **6**: 1–8.
3. Ukers, WH (1935). All about tea. *Tea and Coffee Trade Journal Co.*, New York, USA.
4. Baildon, S (1877). *Tea in Assam*. Calcutta.
5. Barua, DN (1989). *Science and Practice in Tea Culture*. Tea Research Association, Calcutta–Jorhat. p. 493.
6. Griffith, P (1967). *The History of Indian Tea*. Weidenfield and Nicolson, London. p. 730.
7. Ghosh Hajra, N (2001). *Tea Cultivation: Comprehensive Treatise*. Int. Book Distribution Co., Lucknow p. 518.
8. Huang, S (1989). Meteorology of the tea plants in China: A review. *Agric. Forest Meteorol.* 47: 19–30.
9. Hara, Y (2001). *Green Tea: Health Benefits and Application*. Marcel Dekker, Inc., New York. p. 252.

Chapter 2

What is Tea?

The Plant

More than 3,000 different teas are produced in many places around the world and they are all obtained from the same plant species—the *Camellia sinensis* (L.) O. Kuntze[1]. The nomenclature *Camellia sinensis* (L.) was retained for *C. sinensis* var. *sinensis* (L.), but Wight[2] named *C. sinensis* var. *assamica* as *C. assamica*. A third form described as the southern form of tea[3] or Cambod race which resembles Planchon's *Thea lasiocalyx*[4], was proposed by Wight[2] to be a sub-species of *C. assamica* and named *C. assamica* subsp *lasiocalyx* (Planchon ex Watt). The tea varieties have developed into a complex taxonomic group of related plants. A fourth group called 'hybrid variety' with mixed taxonomic characters occupies the largest tea area under cultivation. It propagates by seeds[5]. Tea is essentially an out breeding crop and its races are highly infertile. As a result of enormous natural hybridisation not only between the tea species but also with *Camellias* and large-scale dispersal of tea seeds in south-east Asia over the centuries there is extreme heterogeneity in the existing seedling population.

The tea plant under natural conditions is an evergreen tree and wildly grows into a medium sized tree. Under cultivation, it is pruned down and trained as a low spreading bush to ensure that a maximum crop of young shoots can be obtained and maintained. The root system of a tea bush can be divided into main roots, subsidiary roots and feeder roots. The lateral roots give rise to a surface mat of feeding roots which lack root hairs when mature. Root system varies in tea bushes depending on the genetic make-up and soil environment. Starch is stored in roots.

The tea plant prefers warm temperatures, humidity and plenty of rainfall. The finest teas grow at elevations over 4,000 ft (1,342 m) where cool temperatures in the early morning and evening slow the rate at which new shoots are pushed out, the intense heat during the day encourages the development of flavour in the leaves, and where the clouds that swirl around mountain peaks feed the plant with the moisture that they love.

In tea, the tender apical portions of shoots comprising the terminal bud, the internodes and two or three expanding leaves immediately below it, which together constitute the crop, the 'flush' (2.1) is removed at periodic intervals (Fig. 2.2). It has been worked out that harvesting (plucking) the first two leaves together

Fig. 2.1. Tender Shoots—Flush

with the unfurled bud (Fig. 2.3) is the best compromise between the conflicting demands of high yield and high quality. The time interval in days between pluckings is known as the 'plucking round'. This has a cardinal role in harvesting maximum crop without impairing the quality. The tea pluckers or pickers carry the plucked leaves in baskets or bags on their backs and at the end the leaves are transported to the factory for processing or manufacturing.

Types of Tea and Processing

Tea is generally categorised into three different types—black, green and oolong. Black tea is consumed in the Western hemisphere, while the consumption of green tea is confined mainly to Asia and the Middle East. The worldwide black tea production is about 78 per cent, whereas green tea constitutes about 20 per cent and the rest about 2 per cent is oolong tea. Oolong is mainly produced in China and Taiwan. Small quantities of green and oolong are also produced in India and Sri Lanka.

Fig. 2.2. Tea pluckers in a Darjeeling tea estate

Fig. 2.3. Two leaves and the unfurled bud

Black Tea

Manufacturing processes vary from country to country, but there are two basic methods—orthodox and CTC (cut, tear and curl). All black teas, both orthodox and CTC, go through four basic stages—withering, rolling, fermentation (oxidation) and firing.

i. Withering

It is the first stage of tea manufacture. During withering harvested tea flush is evenly spread on the withering troughs which are normally four to five feet wide and 50 to 70 feet long (Fig. 2.4). During the process, hot and

Fig. 2.4. Plucked tea leaves on withering trough

Fig. 2.5. Rolling machines inside an orthodox tea factory

cold air is blown across the flush to remove the moisture of fresh leaf which is achieved during a 16 to 24 hour period.

ii. Rolling

This process has two objectives: to reduce the leaves into small pieces and to disrupt the leaf structure, so that the polyphenol oxidase is brought into contact with the flavonols and the fermentation can proceed efficiently.

In case of the 'orthodox' type of tea, the withered leaf is charged in the rollers which vary in size (Fig. 2.5). Normally they are 36" and 48" rollers capable of rolling 70 to 120 kg of withered leaf. The pressure is exerted on the leaf in 'open and pressure' sequence. This operation lasts for about 45 minutes. During this process, the tea leaf is twisted as a result of repeated rolling action and simultaneously leaf tissue ruptures thus forcing out the cell sap which spreads as a thin film on the surface of the leaf. Various enzymes and their substrates come in contact and enzymatic oxidation starts at this stage and imparts liquoring properties to the leaves, i.e., briskness, brightness, colour, strength and quality. Moreover, in case of orthodox tea manufacture, this process imparts twist or style to the tea. The green colour of the leaf starts diminishing and a brown coppery colour begins to appear.

The CTC (cut, tear and curl) machine has two rollers with teeth which rotate in opposite directions at different speeds. The teeth mesh in with one another, leaving a gap that is variable. Leaves are drawn through the gap and are cut and curled. It is common practice to reduce the size of the leaves fed to a CTC machine by prior passage through a rotorvane. The cut leaves often pass through a second CTC machine. These machines reduce the leaves to much smaller pieces than those described earlier. This is important for the fine tea required for tea bags (Fig. 2.6). The tea leaves are moved up to the top of the machine by the inclined moving belt. The cutters are behind the top of the inclined belt guards. The tea falls between the pair of cutters. The first machine on the right discharges cut leaf on to the feed belt of the second machine.

Fig. 2.6. CTC machines in a tea processing factory

Fig. 2.7. Rolled leaf on racks

iii. Fermentation (Oxidation)

It is mainly an enzymatic process during which polyphenols are oxidised with the help of enzyme and oxygen from the air. The main objective is to complete the chemical change up to the required degree so that the best balance of liquoring properties is obtained to make the tea liquor pleasant to taste. Rolled leaf is put on racks specially made of tiles (Fig. 2.7), cement or aluminium. Oxidation rooms should be kept clean and cool. In Darjeeling, oxidation is carried out at low temperatures. During hot season, the air is kept humid with the help of humidifiers with less than 20°c hydrometric difference. Optimum oxidation is adjudged by the subjective assessment of the tea maker. Oxidation period varies from two to three hours depending on the type of leaf, degree of wither, temperature, availability of oxygen and oxidising ability of the tea flush. The time of oxidation is reckoned from the time at which rolling begins. Oxidation is a very sensitive process. Even a little longer oxidation period than the optimum is likely to deteriorate the flavour greatly.

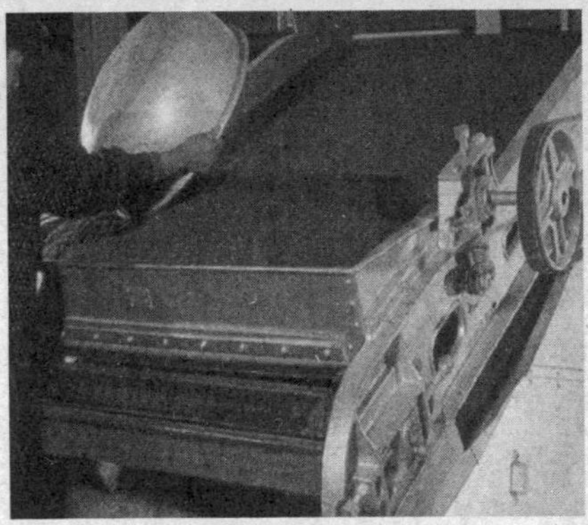

Fig. 2.8. Multi-band Drier

During oxidation the leaf changes colour and becomes dark coppery. A typical aroma develops at this stage. Oxidation sof catechin/polyphenols by the enzyme polyphenol oxidase is the main reaction of the process that imparts 'tea character' to the black tea.

iv. Firing/Drying

The main objective of drying tea are to stop the enzymatic mellowness of fermented leaf so that the desirable mellowness of resultant tea is obtained, and to reduce the moisture of fermented leaf to 2.5 to 3 per cent. Thickness of spread, speed of trays and volume of air blown through are regulated meticulously so as to achieve the correct drying. The whole process of drying is completed within 20 to 30 minutes (Fig. 2.8). Darjeeling teas are normally fired at high temperature which is considered essential for squeezing the correct balance of volatile flavoury compounds in high quality teas.

v. Sorting and Grading

At the end of the manufacturing process, the leaf

particles are sorted into different sizes or 'grades'. Bulk tea is sorted on mechanically oscillated sieves. One of the objectives of sorting is to classify the tea as per the size of the particles. The sieve size decreases gradually from top to bottom. Thus, the bigger leaf size teas are retained on the top while the broken leaves fall towards the floor (Fig. 2.9). The modern sorting machines employ different sieves of varying mesh sizes.

Teas are passed through electrostatically charged rollers (Fig. 2.10) which attract the fibre and stock preferentially. Thus a series of clean teas, free of stalk and fibre are produced. In general, there are four grades

Fig. 2.9. Multi-deck sloping type of sorting machine

Fig. 2.10. Fibre-removing rollers

of tea—whole leaf, broken leaf, fannings and dust. Each of these grades are again classified into various sub-grades. The key grades of black tea are: CTC grades—BP1, BP (Broken Pekoe), PF1, PF (Pekoe Fannings), PD (Pekoe Dust), D1, D; Orthodox grades – TGFOP (Tippy Golden Flowery Orange Pekoe), GFOP, FOP, OP; Brokens – TGBOP (Tippy Golden Broken Orange Pekoe), GBOP, FBOP (Flowery Broken Orange Pekoe); Fannings —BOPF, GOF, Dust—PD, D1, etc.

Green Tea

The plucked leaves are laid out in the sun or in the warm air of the factory and are allowed to wither until they are slightly limp and soft. The leaves are then heat-treated to destroy any enzymes that would react with the oxygen in the air and cause the leaf to rot. Green teas are therefore known as unoxidised teas. Heat is applied either by pan-frying in a large wok, as in China, or by steaming, as in Japan. The fresh green leaves are steamed to kill the oxidising enzymes allowing the final product to stay green. The steamed tea is then alternately rolled and dried, but allowed to retain 3 per cent moisture. Steaming is the common practice in Assam, whereas in Uttaranchal and Kangra valley the leaves are pan fried. In India, rolling is done in a conventional roller unlike the Japanese process in which the rolling is done in a drum. Green tea leaves give straw-coloured or pale greenish-yellow or brownish-yellow liquor and generally have a somewhat astringent or pungent flavour. The common grades of green tea are: Fine Young Hyson, Young Hyson, Hyson No. 1, Twanky, Fannings or Soumee, and Dust.

Oolong Tea

This tea is often called semi-fermented or semi-oxidised tea and is principally produced in the Fujian province of China, and in Taiwan. The time of picking is crucial for the production of quality oolong tea—the leaves should be neither too young nor too mature. The leaves are wilted for four to five hours in direct sunlight or in warm air inside the factory to remove some percentage of the water content. The leaves are then rolled and allowed to react with oxygen in the air. The leaves start to give off a smell similar to orchids or peaches. The colour of the leaf gradually changes. The centre of the leaf remains a yellowish green while the edges, where the enzymes have oxidised, become reddish brown. The processed leaf is heated in either to pans or ovens to stop oxidation and allowed to retain 3 per cent moisture content. This tea produces a strawberry coloured liquor.

White Tea

It is an unfermented tea made from very young tea leaves or buds that are steamed immediately after harvest to inactivate polyphenol oxidase and then dried. Consequently, white teas usually contain higher concentrations of catechins than other teas. Tiny silver hairs that cover the buds give the tea a white appearance. White teas are the rarest in the world, produced on a very limited scale in China and Sri Lanka. These teas are traditionally plucked only at daybreak in the four provinces of north-east Fujian, so that the buds are unopened.

Decaffeinated Tea

Lifestyle trends are changing and as consumers today

become more health conscious, there is demand for decaffeinated tea. Caffeine is removed by treating the tea with organic solvents, viz. methylene chloride, ethyl acetate, and super critical carbon dioxide. Methyl chloride is the cheapest and is most easily removed from the tea after the decaffeination process. But the US and

How to Brew the Perfect Cup of Hot Tea

The process of tea making varies and mainly depends on the taste of the consumer. However, experts in tea recommend a few golden rules for the brewing of perfect teas. Different types of teas need different water temperature and different infusion times. Use only freshly boiled water to pour over the tea leaves. Warm the teapot by rinsing with hot water. One small teaspoon of good quality tea per cup is a rough estimate. Infuse for two minutes. For Darjeeling tea, let it seep for four to five minutes before straining. Add milk and sugar to taste. Stir and sip. Green tea should always be made with water that has been boiled and allowed to cool for a few minutes to a temperature of between 70°C and 90°C (158°F and 194°F).

Box 2.1

Germany have banned all imports of products using methyl chloride. Carbon dioxide is most widely used and is thought to be the least harmful. However, decaffeinated tea is not totally free of caffeine. After decaffeination, a small percentage of caffeine still remains in the leaf.

Instant Tea

It can be made with black tea leaf, (partially) fermented, undried leaf, oolong or green tea. Tea infusion is evaporated and the solid so formed is dried and powdered and infused again to get the liquor which is known as instant tea. It is also known as powdered tea. Instant tea is produced in India, Sri Lanka, Kenya, and exported mainly to the USA and UK. Instant tea is also produced in USA in fairly large quantities from black tea as raw material. Instant tea is mainly used as a component of iced drinks in USA.

Organic Tea

The aim of organic tea producers is to grow a crop of high nutritional quality in sufficient quantity, encourage and enhance biological cycles within the farming system; involve micro-organisms, soil flora and fauna, plants and animals; maintain and increase the long-term fertility of soils; use on-farm resources in locally organised agricultural systems; avoid all forms of pollution that may result from agricultural techniques; ensure an adequate return, a safe working environment and the long term well-being of the planet. Cultivation under organic system is rigidly controlled by the certification bodies which act as a trust building system between producers and customers, help in authentication of product, enable transparency, strengthen the position of the primary producer and helps in market promotion of product. The certification includes inspection at all stages of production and marketing.

Organic tea is a value added product. Demand for this tea has been growing rapidly since it was introduced in the world market in the late 1980s. Reflecting this strong demand, organically grown teas command a premium of 30–40 per cent over conventionally produced teas[6].

Flavoured Tea

The craze among today's young generation is to drink flavoured teas, especially in the United States. This has led the major blending companies to create very wide range of flavoured tea varieties. Flavoured teas are also popular in Denmark, France and Germany. Traditionally, jasmine tea is made by exposing green tea (or light oolong) to fresh jasmine at night when the flowers are most fragrant. They are then separated during the day. This process is repeated several times. This is the one flavoured tea in which high qualities of both tea and jasmine are occasionally used to create a wonderful beverage. Other flavoured teas are made by adding essential oils (bergamot for early grey), herbs, spices, perfumes or even synthetic flavourings. Although the flavoured tea satisfies the consumer to a certain extent, it is, however, yet to be established.

Spiced Tea

Spiced tea or *Masala chai* is an aromatic spiced tea, which has been the Indian drink of choice for years. Freshly ground spices like ginger, cinnamon, cardamom, nutmeg and cloves are added to a boiling pot of water, loose leaf tea, sugar and milk, to make a hot, delicious, nutritious, and satisfying beverage (Fig.2.11). Due to the remarkable popularity of *masala chai* worldwide—from Toronto to Tokyo and Seattle to Stockholm—this aspect of creative and vivid expression and articulation of Indian culture finds amazing outpourings throughout the world.

Fig. 2.11. Tea leaves being boiled with water, milk, sugar and spices.

Herbal Tea

Herbal tea is not actually made from *Camellia sinensis*, but is rather a herb or a mixture of herbs. Herbal tea is a different product altogether. The only factor it shapes with tea is that it is also made with boiling water. Its use, until the last decade, was largely therapeutic and its distribution was limited to the health food trade. Only in the United States are these herbal mixtures called tea. They are usually referred to as an infusion or tisane in other parts of the world. Among the dozens of herbal teas available in the market are: Camomile, Peppermint, Rosehip, Matte, Fennel, Nettle Lemon, Morning blend,

Night blend, Orange, Lemon, Cherry, Strawberry, Raspberry, and Blackcurrant to name a few.

References

1. Jane Pettigrew (1999). *Tea*, PRC Publishing Ltd., London. p. 96.
2. Wight, W (1962). Tea classification revised, *Current Sci.* **31**: 298–299.
3. Roberts, EAH, Wight, W and Wood, DJ (1958). Paper chromatography as an aid to the identification of *Thea camellia*. *New Phytologist* **57**: 221–225.
4. Barua, PK (1963). Classification of the tea plant. *Two and a Bud* **10**: 3–11.
5. Wight, W (1958). The agrotype concept in tea taxonomy. *Nature* **181**: 893–895.
6. Ghosh Hajra, N (2002). Organic tea growing in Darjeeling hills: An overview. *Pestology* **26**: 11–26.

Chapter 3

Tea Chemistry and Antioxidative Effects

Tea Chemistry

Black and green teas are produced from the leaves of *Camellia sinensis*. The difference between them lies in the manufacturing process. Although the chemical composition of tea varies with climate, season, variety, cultivation practices, and the age of the leaves[1], the major green tea polyphenols are: (-)-epigallocatechin-3-gallate (EGCG), (-)-epigallocatechin (EGC), (-)-epicatechin-3-gallate (ECG), and (-)-epicatechin (EC) (Fig. 3.1). EC has an ortho-dihydroxyl group in the B-ring at carbons 3' and 4' and a hydroxyl group at carbon 3 on the C ring. EGC differs from EC in that it has a trihydroxyl group at carbons 3', 4', and 5' on the B ring and a gallate moiety esterified at carbon 3 on the C ring. EGCG is the major catechin in tea accounting for more than 10 per cent on a dry weight basis. Catechin, gallocatechin, epigallocatechin digallates, epicatechin digallates, 3–*0*–methyl EC and EGC, catechin gallate, and gallocatechin gallate are present in smaller quantities. Catechins are colourless, water-soluble bioactive compounds[2]. Flavonols including quercetin, kaempferol, myricitin, rutin and their glycosides, are also present in tea[3]. Black teas typically contain one-third the level of catechins present in green teas (Fig. 3.2). Back teas additionally contains complex oligomeric and polymeric polyphenols, theaflavins (TF) and thearubigins (TR), which are formed during processing as products of polyphenol oxidase-mediated catechin oxidation[4]. The major TF in black teas are theaflavin (TF1), theaflavin-3-gallate (TF2A), theaflavin–3′–gallate (TF2B), and theaflavin–3, 3′–digallate (TF3)[5] (Fig. 3.3). Chemistry of thearubigins is highly complex and their structures have not yet been established. If the TFs start getting oxidised to TRs, it has a deleterious effect on the quality of tea.

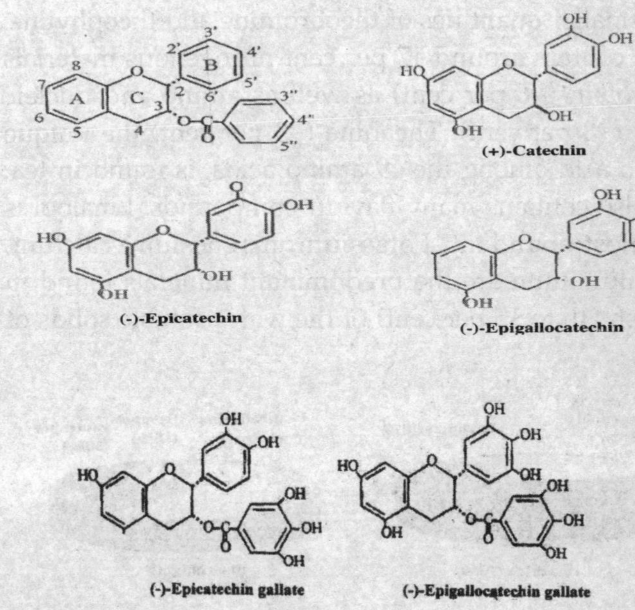

Fig. 3.1. Structure and nomenclature of the principal catechins found in tea

Tea is the largest beverage by volume (800 billion litres)

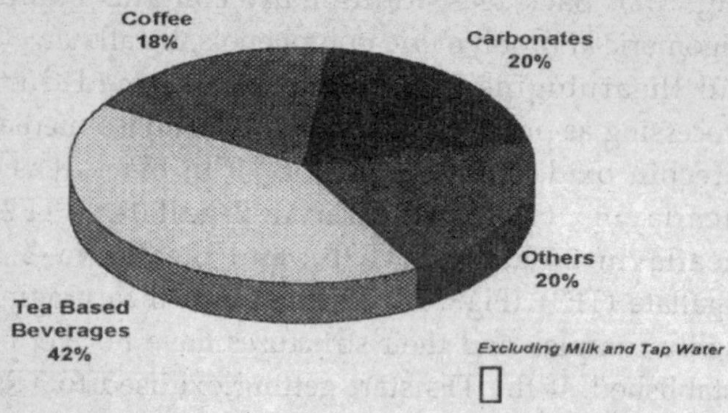

Box 3.1

Source: Ref. 60

Tea leaves contain about 3 to 6 per cent caffeine and smaller quantities of theobromine and theophyline. They contain around 17 per cent nitrogenous materials as protein (~6 per cent) as well as amino and nucleic acids (~8 per cent). Theanine (~3 per cent) the unique amino acid among the 19 amino acids, is found in tea. Tea also contains many flavour compounds. Linalool is the most abundant. Potassium, magnesium, calcium, and aluminum are the predominant minerals found in the ash (10 to 15 per cent) of the water-soluble solids of tea.

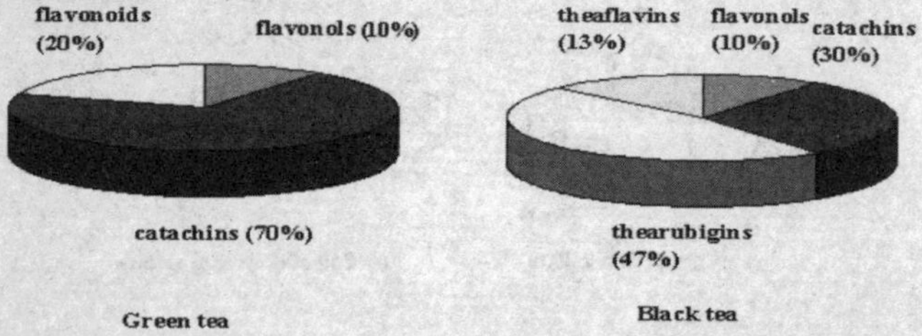

Fig. 3.2. Typical flavonoids composition of green and black tea

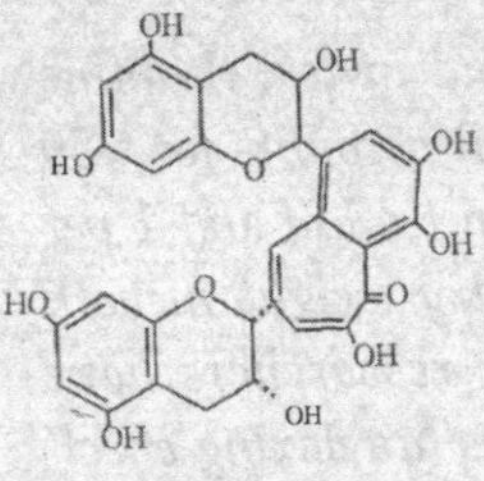

Theaflavin

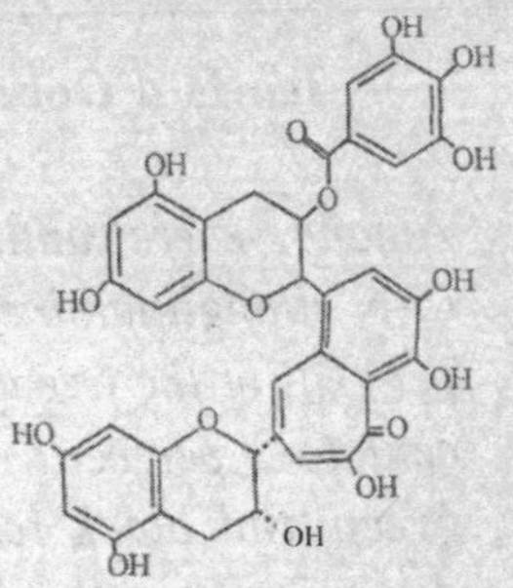

Theaflavin 3'-gallate

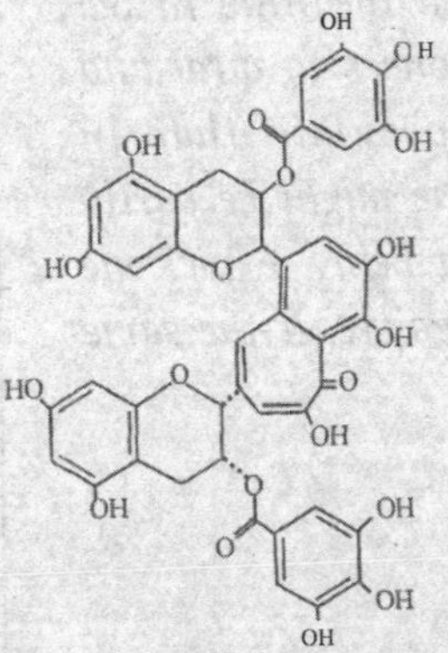

Theaflavin 3, 3'-digallate

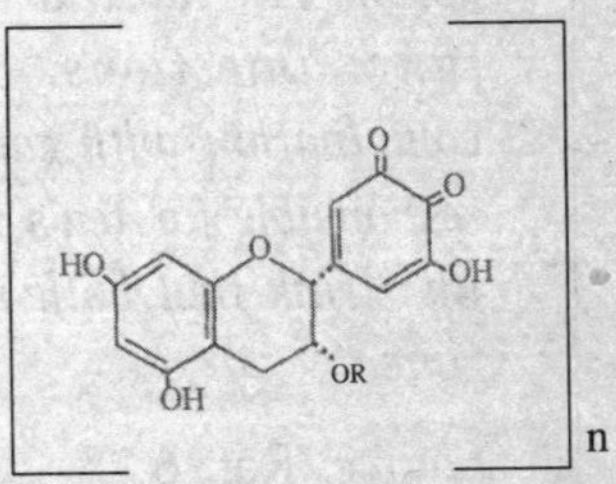

Thearubigins

Fig. 3.3. Theaflavins and thearubigins

Antioxidative Effects of Tea

Tea is an important source of flavonoids in the diet[7] providing almost 200 mg/cup in case of a typical brew of black tea[8]. The flavonoid concentration of any particular tea beverage depends upon the type of tea (e.g., blended, decaffeinated or instant) and preparation (e.g., amount used, brew time and temperature)[9]. The highest concentration of flavonoids is found in brewed hot tea (541–692 µg/ml), less in instant preparations (90–100 µg/ml) and the lowest in iced and ready-to-drink

Tea Is a Good Source of Amino Acids

Among several amino acids found in tea, theanine (5-N-ethylglutamine) is unique. It accounts for >50 per cent of the free amino acids in tea leaf and 1 per cent to 2 per cent of the total dry weight in both green and black teas. Japanese researchers have discovered that this compound has 'a relaxing effect' on humans, based in increased alpha wave activity. Additional research has indicated theanine in tea assists our natural immune responses to viral and fungi infections. Scientists speculate that in combination with caffeine, theanine might be partly responsible for tea's reputation for being a 'pick-me up' drink that both relaxes and revives at the same time.

Source: Ref. 6

Box 3.2

teas[10, 11]. Decaffeination reduces the catechin content of black tea by 10–20 per cent[1]. The most important property of almost every group of flavonoids is their capacity to act as antioxidants. The flavones and catechins seem to be the most powerful flavonoids for protecting the body against reactive oxygen species[12]. Body cells and tissues are continuously threatened by the damage caused by free radicals and reactive oxygen species. Free radicals are molecules that possess unpaired electrons. These molecules are in a constant state of instability as they are constantly trying to pair up their electrons resulting in their high reactivity. Oxygen radicals such as super oxide anion radical ($O_2^{\bullet}$–), singlet oxygen ($^1O_2$), and hydroxyl radical ($^{\bullet}OH$) in particular, which are naturally generated in the body as a result of chemical reactions during normal cellular processes, also are highly reactive. They can also be formed in response to excess pollution, too much UV sunlight and exposure to cigarette smoke. In an attempt to stabilise, they attack other molecules in the body potentially leading to cell damage [13] and triggering the formation of another free radical resulting in a chain reaction. It is believed that this type of free radical action has been implicated in certain chronic diseases such as cancer, heart disease [14], stroke, rheumatoid arthritis and ageing. Free radicals not only react with lipids to produce degenerative lipid peroxides, but they also attack DNA or other organic constituents to induce various oxidative damage[15]. The generation of radical oxygens and their actions, defence systems against them, the role of antioxidative flavonoids in relation to diseases and ageing have been extensively researched[16].

The antioxidant activity of green tea epicatechin (GTE) and its epimers in canned and bottled tea drinks was conducted in three *in vitro* systems, namely human LDL (low density lipoproteins) oxidation, ferric reducing–antioxidant power (FRAP), and anti–2, 2–diphenyl–1–picrylhydrazyl (DPPH) free radical assays[17]. It was demonstrated that catechin gallate (CG) had similar antioxidant capacity as its precursor epicatechin gallate (ECG) while gallocatechin (GC) was less potent as an antioxidant than its precursor epigallocatechin (EGC). Regarding epigallocatechin gallate (EGCG) and gallocatechin gallate (GCG), the antioxidant potency was similar for both LDL oxidation and DPPH free radical assays, but GCG was statistically less effective than EGCG in the FRAP assay. For epicatechin (EC) and catechin, the latter had less anti-free radical activity in the DPPH assay, but antioxidant activity was found similar in LDL oxidation and FRAP assays. In general, both ECs and epimers had low bioavailability and most of the observed differences between epicatechins and their corresoponding epimers were small. It was also concluded that the epimerisation reaction occurring during the manufacturing of canned and bottled tea drinks did not significantly affect antioxidant activity and bioavailability of total tea polyphenols[17].

Tea flavonoids are potent antioxidants that are absorbed from the gut after consumption and significantly increase the antioxidant capacity of the blood[18].

Tea has greater *in vitro* antioxidant capacity than most fruits and vegetables per serving and tea is more potent than Vitamins C, E, and the carotenoids[19] (Fig. 3.4). The potential health benefits associated with tea consumption have been chiefly attributed to the antioxidative action of tea polyphenols. This has been reviewed by the researchers in the past[20–22].

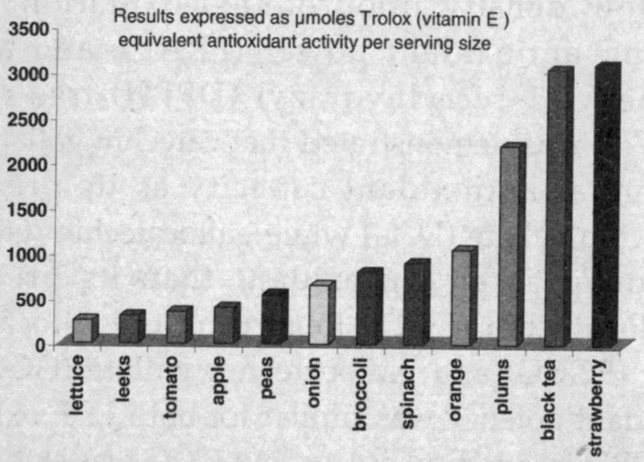

Fig. 3.4. Antioxidant capacity of tea, fruits and vegetables

Potential Mechanisms for the Antioxidant Effects of Tea

Tea polyphenols act as antioxidants *in vitro* by scavenging reactive oxygen and nitrogen species and chelating redox-active transition metal ions. They may also function indirectly as antioxidants through (i) inhibition of the redox-sensitive transcription factors, nuclear factor–kB and activator protein–1; (ii) inhibition of 'pro-oxidant' enzymes, such as inducible nitric oxide synthase, lipoxygenases, cyclooxygenases and xanthine oxidase; and (iii) induction of phase II and antioxidant enzymes, such as glutathione S–transferases and superoxide dismutases.[20–21]

No significant difference in antioxidant activity (lipoprotein oxidation)[23] (total radical scavenging capacity)[24, 25] was found in black and green teas although their compositions are different. But the radical quenching ability of green tea is usually higher than that of black tea[3]. Langley-Evans[26] found the total antioxidant capacity of green tea to be more potent than that of black tea.

i. Scavenging of Reactive Oxygen Species and Reactive Nitrogen Species

Tea catechins and polyphenols have been found to be efficient scavengers of free radicals in a number of *in vitro* systems[27]. The ability of a compound to act as a free radical scavenger is partly related to its one-electron reduction potential, a measure of reactivity of antioxidants as hydrogen or electron donors[28]. A lower reduction potential indicates that lower energy is required for hydrogen or electron donation. EGCG and EGC have lower reduction potentials than vitamin E (Table 3.1), suggesting they are superior electron donors

Table 3.1
Reduction potentials [29, 32, 33] and relative antioxidant activities of tea polyphenols[30] and other antioxidants[28].

Antioxidant	*Reduction potential (V)[a]*	*Antioxidant activity (mM)[b]*
(–)–Epicatechin	0.57	2.4 ± 0.02
(–)–Epicatechin gallate	0.55	4.9 ± 0.02
(–)–Epigallocatechin gallate	0.43	4.8 ± 0.06
(–)–Epigallocatechin	0.43	3.8 ± 0.06
Theaflavin	0.51	2.9 ± 0.08
Theaflavin digallate	0.54	6.2 ± 0.43
Green tea (1000 ppm)	–	3.8 ± 0.03
Black tea (1000 ppm)	–	3.5 ± 0.03
Viamin E	0.48	1.0 ± 0.03
Vitamin C	0.28	1.0 ± 0.02

[a]Reduction potential at pH 7, 20°C
[b]TEAC (Trolox equivalent antioxidant activity)

to vitamin E[29]. Vitamin C has a significantly lower reduction potential, indicating it is superior to all tea polyphenols measured. In addition to hydrogen or electron donating activity, the effectiveness of an antioxidant is also determined by the rate of its reaction with free radicals in a given system (scavenging rate constant) and the stability of the resulting antioxidant radical[20].

ii. Metal chelation

The ability of tea polyphenols to chelate metal ions, such as iron and copper, may contribute to their antioxidant activity by preventing redox-active transition metals from catalysing free radicals formation.[30] These metal chelating properties likely explain the ability of tea polyphenols to inhibit copper-mediated LDL oxidation and other transition metal-catalysed oxidations *in vitro*[31].

(iii) Inhibition of Redox-sensitive Transcription Factors

Green and black tea, as well as individual catechins and tea polyphenols, can inhibit the activation of the redox-sensitive transcription factors, nuclear factor – kB (NF-kB) and activator protein–1 (AP–1), in cultured cells. Although other antioxidants can also inhibit these redox-sensitive transcription factors, recent research indicates that tea catechins and polyphenols are acting as kinase inhibitors in complex signalling pathways[21]. However, the kinase inhibiting activities of tea polyphenols may not be directly related to their ability to function as hydrogen donators or antioxidants[3].

(iv) Inhibition of 'pro-oxidant' Enzymes

The inhibition of enzymes whose activity may increase oxidative stress represents a potential indirect antioxidant effect of tea catechins. Stimulation of inflammatory cells such as macrophages by bacterial endotoxins or inflammatory cytokines results in increased expression of inducible nitric oxide synthase (iNOS) and subsequent production of large amounts of nitric oxide (NO)[21]. Nitric oxide reacts rapidly with $O_2^{\cdot -}$ *in vivo* to form $OONO^-$ and other ·NO-derived oxidants capable of damaging DNA and proteins[34]. Green tea and black tea[35-36], as well as individual catechins[37-38] and theaflavins[39], can inhibit lipopolysaccharide-induced iNOS gene expression and iNOS activity in cultured macrophages. Green tea catechins and black tea theaflavins appear to down regulate iNOS by inhibiting

NF–kB activation[38–39]. Green and black tea polyphenols have been found to inhibit cyclooxygenase and lipoxygenases activities in human colon mucosa cells and human colon cancer cells[40]. Tea polyphenols may also inhibit the formation of reactive oxygen species by inhibiting the enzyme xanthine oxidase.

Xanthin oxidase catalyses the oxidation of both hypoxanthin and xanthine to uric acid while reducing O_2 to $O_2^{\cdot -}$ and H_2O_2.[20, 21] Green tea catechins have been found to inhibit the activity of xanthine oxidase *in vitro*, with EGCG exerting the most potent effect[41]. EGCG from green tea and theaflavins gallates from black tea have also been found to inhibit xanthine oxidase activity in culture human leukemia cells[42].

(v) Induction of Phase II Enzymes

Phase II detoxification enzymes promote the excretion of potentially toxic or carcinogenic chemicals. Most phase II enzymes contain *cis*-acting regulatory elements called antioxidant response elements (ARE)[21]. Glutathione S–transferases (GST) are a family of phase II enzymes that catalyse the conjugation of glutathione to electrophiles, thereby reducing their ability to react with nucleic acids and proteins[43]. Increase in the activity of ARE-mediated reporter gene in transfected HepG2 cells by the extract of green tea polyphenol[44] as well as individual green tea catechins[45] have been reported. Feeding green tea leaves for 63 weeks to rats significantly increased liver GST activity[46]. Inclusion of green tea polyphenols (0.2%) in the drinking water for up to 30 days also significantly increased GST activity in the liver and small intestine of mice[47].

Tea and Health: The Caffeine Issue

Caffeine is an alkaloid (1,3,7-trimethylxanthin) of the purine group, a colourless compound with a slightly bitter taste and has a stimulating effect on human beings. Tea leaves contain about 3 to 6 percent caffeine. One cup of tea (170 ml or 6 oz) contains 25.5 mg to 34 mg of caffeine, i.e. roughly one third of the caffeine found in coffee. Further, the efficacy of caffeine in tea is safe; it does not have the residue poison and the toxic effects, which is the reason as the caffeine in tea rapidly take off the partial methyl, carries on the oxidation process and discharges by 3 methyl-uric acids forms after the organisms absorb in; its residual time in the body does not surpass 24 hours. Therefore, moderate tea consumption will not lead to any potential risk associated with caffeine exposure. Also, of interest to caffeine-sensitive individuals, both tea and decaffeinated tea have been observed to have comparable antioxidant activity.

Canada's Guidelines for Healthy Eating indicate that an excess of 400 mg to 450 mg of caffeine per day (i.e. 15 to 17 cups of tea/day) may only pose some concern.

The effects of caffeine on osteoporosis have been raised by some researchers but recent studies suggest that caffeine does not promote osteoporosis.

Concern regarding caffeine in tea is not an issue as long as tea is consumed in moderation as suggested by Canadian and other health authorities.

Box 3.3

Antioxidant Functions of Tea Catechins

The antioxidant capacity of teas and tea polyphenols has been assessed by several methods.

In order to assess the modifying effect of tea flavonoids on plasma antioxidant status, several assays of total antioxidant capacity have been applied. The FRAP (ferric reducing ability of plasma) assay is based on the reduction of Fe^{3+} ions to Fe^{2+} ions. The TRAP (total radical trapping antioxidant parameter) assays measure total peroxyl radical trapping capacity. The TEAC (trolox equivalent antioxidant capacity) assay is based on the formation and scavenging of the $ATBS^{+}$ radical cation. The ORAC (oxygen radical absorbance capacity) assay is a commonly used TRAP assay that is based on the ability of a test substance to inhibit the oxidation of phycoerythrin by reactive oxygen species, relative to Trolox. Each assay differs somewhat in its measurement of the individual contributions of plasma antioxidants due to the differences in the nature of the radical generating system and the conditions of the assay. Further, the antioxidant capacity of flavonoids determined *in vitro* is dependent upon the type of assay employed and does not reflect factors such as bioavailability and metabolism. Using ORAC assay, Cao and coworkers[48] found that both green and black teas have much higher antioxidant activity against peroxyl radicals than vegetables such as garlic, kale, spinach and Brussels sprouts. Using FRAP assay, the total *ex vivo* antioxidant capacity of green tea was found to be more than that of black tea[26]. Thus, *ex vivo* tests of antioxidant capacity would appear to better represent the physiological impact of tea[10].

Animal studies offer a unique opportunity to assess the contribution of the antioxidant properties of tea and tea polyphenols to the physiological effects of tea administration in different models of oxidative stress. Most promising are the consistent findings in animal models of skin, lung, colon, liver, and pancreatic cancer that tea and tea polyphenol administration inhibits carcinogen-induced increases in the oxidised DNA base, 8–hydroxy–2′–deoxyguanosine[21]. In animal model, green and black tea administration was found to improve the resistance of lipoproteins to *ex vivo* oxidation, the improvement was much less than that conferred by supplementation with other antioxidants. Very limited data suggest that green tea or ECGC administration may protect protein from oxidative damage[21]. Recently, involvement of oxidative stress in

Table 3.2
Effect of tea consumption on plasma antioxidant capacity in human intervention studies

Assay	*Plasma antioxidant capacity*	*Reference*
TRAP	[+ 4% (GT), + 3% (BT)] ns	50
TRAP	+ 34% (GT), + 29% (BT)	51
ECL	No effect (BT)	52
TEAC	+ 3% (GT), no effect (BT)	53
ECL	No effect (BT)	54
FRAP	+ 4% (GT)	55
FRAP	+ 3% (GT), + 2% (BT)	56
TEAC	+ 12.7% (GT)	57
FRAP	+ 76% (BT)	58
FRAP	[+ 12% (BT)] ns	59
ORAC	[+ 11% (BT)] ns	59

TRAP = total radical trapping antioxidant parameters; ECL = enhanced chemiluminescence; TEAC = trolox equivalent antioxidant capacity; FRAP = ferric reducing antioxidant power; ORAC = oxygen radical absorbance capacity; BT = black tea; GT = green tea; ns = non-significant.

hypertension in stroke-prone spontaneously hypertensive rats (SHRSP) has been reported[49]. The data demonstrate that both black and green tea polyphenols attenuate increase of blood pressure through their antioxidant properties in SHRSP. It was further suggested, because the amounts of polyphenols used in this experiment correspond to those in ~1 L of tea, the regular consumption of black and green tea may also provide some protection against hypertension in humans.

A substantial number of human intervention studies (Table 3.2) with green and black tea demonstrated a significant increase in plasma antioxidant capacity in humans ~ 1 h after consumption of moderate amounts of tea (1–6 cups/day). There are initial indications that the enhanced blood antioxidant potential leads to reduced oxidative damage to macromolecules such as DNA and lipids. However, the measurement of oxidative damage through biomarkers needs to be further established[18]. Although scientific support is strongest for the protection of DNA from oxidative damage after consumption of black and green tea but the number of studies now available are not sufficient to draw firm conclusion. Therefore, further research on the measurements of oxidative damage biomarkers, stimulation of the body's own antioxidant defence systems by tea flavonoids, increased gene expression of antioxidant responsive elements and subsequently enhanced expression and activity of detoxifying enzymes in human intervention studies are suggested[18].

Reasons for Difference in Results of Animal and Human Studies

Although the consumption of tea or tea polyphenols results in modest transient increases in plasma antioxidant capacity in humans, limited research has not generally revealed significant decreases in biomarkers of in vivo oxidative damage[20]. The concentrations of tea used in animal and human studies are often similar, but animals generally receive much higher doses relative to body weight than humans. Findings that tea or tea polyphenols administration inhibits increases in 8-OHdG induced by chemical carcinogens provide the most consistent evidence that tea and tea polyphenols have antioxidant effects in vivo. In contrast, observational studies in humans do not generally support a significant chemopreventive effect of black or green tea consumption. [20] Although observational studies in humans have a number of limitations, it is also possible that animal models employing chemical carcinogens may not be entirely relevant to the causes of oxidative stress and cancer in humans. While genetic variability is limited in animal models, wide genetic variations in the response of humans to oxidative stress may obscure small changes in biomarkers induced by tea polyphenols. To determine whether increased consumption of tea or tea polyphenols prevents oxidative damage to biomolecules and associated pathology in humans, research in humans and animals should employ sensitive and specific markers of oxidative damage to lipids, proteins and DNA, such as

F_{2}-isoprostanes, protein carbonyls and the comet assay. To increase the applicability of data from animal studies, the likely sources of oxidative stress and associated diseases in humans should be relevant to the animal models selected to assess the antioxidant activity of tea polyphenols[21].

Box 3.4

References

1. Graham, HN (1992). Green tea composition, consumption, and polyphenol chemistry. *Prev. Med.* **21**: 334–350.
2. Arts, ICW, Hollman, PCH, Feskens, EJM, Mesquita, HBB and Kromhout, D (2001). Catechin intake and associated dietary and lifestyle factors in a representative sample of Dutch men and women. *Eur. J. Clinical Nutr.* **55**: 76–81.
3. Yang, CS, Maliakal, P and Meng, X (2002). Inhibition of carcinogenesis by tea. *Annu. Rev. Pharmacol. Toxicol.* **42**: 25–54.
4. Wiseman, SA, Mulder, T and Rietveld, A (2001). Tea flavonoids: Bioavailability *in vivo* and effects on cell signalling pathways *in vitro*. *Antioxidants & Redox Signalling* **3**: 1009–1021.
5. Su, YL, Leung, LK, Huang, Y and Chen, Z–Y (2003). Stability of tea theaflavins and catechins. *Food Chemistry* **83**: 189–195.
6. Anonymous 2003. Tea & Health. *Tea & Coffee Asia* **5**: 27–29.
7. McKay, DL and Blumberg, JB (2002). The role of tea in human health: An update. *J. Am. Coll. Nutr.* **21**: 1–13.
8. Lakenbrink, C, Lapczynski, S, Maiwald, B and Engelhardt, UH (2000). Flavonoids and other polyphenols in consumer brews of tea and other caffeinated beverages. *J. Agric. Food Chem.* **48**: 2848-2852.
9. Blumberg, J (2003). Introduction to the proceedings of the third international scientific symposium on tea and human health: Role of flavonoids in diet. *J. Nutr.* **133**: 3244S–3246S.

10. Hakim, I, Weisgerber, U, Harris, R, Balentine, D, van-Mierlo, C. and Paetau-Robinson, I (2000). Preparation, composition and consumption patterns of tea-based beverages in Arizona. *Nutr. Res.* **20**: 1715–1724.
11. Arts, I, van De Putte, B and Hollman, O (2000). Catechin contents of foods commonly consumed in the Netherlands. 2. Tea, wine, fruit juices and chocolate milk. *J. Agric. Food Chem.* **48**:1752–1757.
12. Nijveldt, RJ, Nood, EV, van Hoorn, DEC, Boelens, PG, Norren, KV and van Leeuwen, PAM (2001). Flavonoids: A review of probable mechanisms of action and potential applications. *Am. J. Clin. Nutr.* **74**: 418–425.
13. de Groot H (1994). Reactive oxygen species in tissue injury. *Hepatogastroenterology* **41**: 328–332.
14. Grace, PA (1994). Ischaemia-reperfusion injury. *Br. J. Surg.* **81**: 637–647.
15. Hara, Y (2001) *Green Tea: Health Benefits and Applications.* Marcel Dekker Inc., New York, p. 252.
16. Rice-Evans, CA and Packer, L (1998). *Flavonoids in Health and Disease.* (ed.) Marcel Dekker Inc., New York.
17. Xu, Jin Z, Yeung, SYV, Chang, Q, Huang, Y and Chen, Z–Y (2004). Comparison of antioxidant activity and bioavailability of tea epicatechins with their epimers. *British J. Nutr.* **91**: 873–881.
18. Rietveld, A and Wiseman, S (2003). Antioxidant effects of tea: evidence from human clinical trials. *J. Nutr.* **133**: 3285S–3292S.
19. Wiseman, SA, Balentine, DA and Frei, B (1997). Antioxidants in tea. *Crit. Rev. Food Sci. Nutr.* **37**: 705–718.
20. Higdon, JV and Frei, B (2003). Tea catechins and polyphenols: Health effects, metabolism, and antioxidant functions. *Critical Rev. Food Sci. Nutr.* **43**: 89–143.
21. Frei, B and Higdon, V (2003). Antioxidant activity of tea polyphenols *in vitro*: evidence from animal studies. *J. Nutr.* **133**: 3275S–3284S.
22. Siddiqi, IA, Afaq, F, Adhami, VM, Ahmad, M and Mukhtar, H (2004). Antioxidants of the beverage tea in promotion of human health. *Antioxidants and Redox Signalling* **6**: 571–582.

23. Hodgson, JM, Proudfoot, JM, Croft, KD, Puddey, IB, Mori, TA and Beilin, LJ (1999). Comparison of the effects of black and green tea on *in vitro* lipoprotein oxidation in human serum. *J. Sci. Food Agric.* **79**: 561–566.
24. Toit, RD, Volsteedt, Y and Apostolides, Z (2001). Comparison of the antioxidant content of fruits, vegetables and teas measured as vitamin C equivalent. *Toxicology* **166**: 63–69.
25. Leung, LK, Su, Y, Chen, R, Zhang, Z, Huang, Y and Chen, Zhen-Yu (2001). Theaflavins in black tea and catechins in green tea are equally effective antioxidants. *J. Nutr.* **131**: 2248–2251.
26. Langley-Evans, S (2000). Antioxidant potential of green and black tea determined using the ferric reducing power (FRAP) assay. *Int. J. Food Sci. Nutr.* **51**: 181–188.
27. Rice-Evans, C (1999). Implications of the mechanism of action of tea polyphenols as antioxidants *in vitro* for chemoprevention in humans. *Proc. Soc. Exp. Biol.* Med. **220**: 262–266.
28. Helliwel, B and Gutteridge, JMC 1999. *Free Radicals in Biology Medicine*. 3rd ed., Oxford University Press, New York.
29. Jovanavic, SV, Steenken, S and Simic, MG (1996). Reduction potentials of flavonoid and model phenoxyl radicals. *J. Chem. Soc. Perkins Trans.* **2**: 2497–2503.
30. Rice-Evans, CA, Miller, NJ and Paganga, G (1997). Antioxidant properties of phenolic compounds. *Trends Plant Sci.* **2**: 152–159.
31. Brown, JE, Khodr, H, Hider, RC and Rice-Evans, CA (1998). Structural dependence of flavonoid interactions with Cu 2+ ions: Implications for their antioxidant properties. *Biochem. J.* **330**: 1173–1178.
32. Anderson, RF, Fisher, LJ, Hara, Y, Harris, T, Mak, WB, Melton, LD and Packer, JE (2001). Green tea catechins partially protect DNA from OH radical-induced strand breaks and base damage through fast chemical repair of DNA radicals. *Carcinogenesis* **22**: 1189-1193.
33. Jovanavic, SV, Hara, Y., Steenken, S. and Simic, MG 1995. Antioxidant potential of gallocatechins. A pulse radiolysis laser photolysis study. *J. Am. Chem. Soc.* **117**: 9881–9888.

34. Surh, YJ, Chun, KS, Cha, HH., Han, SS, Keum, YS, Park, KK and Lee, SS (2001). Molecular mechanisms underlying chemopreventive activities of anti-inflammatory phytochemicals: Down regulation of COX-2 and iNOS through suppression of NF-kappa B activation. *Mutat. Res.* **480–481**: 243–268.
35. Paquay, JB, Haenen, GR, Stender, G, Wiseman, SA, Tijburg, LB and Bast, A (2000). Protection against nitric oxide toxicity by tea. *J. Agric. Food Chem.* **48**: 5768–5772.
36. Sarker, A and Bhaduri, A (2001). Black tea is a powerful chemopreventor of reactive oxygen and nitrogen species: comparison with its individual catechin constituents and green tea. *Biochem. Biophys. Res. Commun.* **284**: 173–178.
37. Chan MM, Fong, D, Ho, CT and Huang, HI (1997). Inhibition of inducible nitric oxide synthase gene expression and enzyme activity by epigallocatechin gallate, a natural product from green tea. *Biochem. Pharmacol.* **54**: 1281–1286.
38. Lin, YL and Lin, JK 1997. (-)-Epigallocatechin-3-gallate blocks the induction of nitric oxide synthase by down-regulating lipopolysaccharide-induced activity of transcription factor nuclear factor-kappaB. *Mol. Pharmacol.* **52**: 465–472.
39. Lin, YL, Tsai, SH, Lin–Shiau, SY, Ho, CT and Lin, JK (1999). Theaflavin-3, 3′-digallate from black tea blocks the nitric oxide synthase by down-regulating the activation of NF-kappaB in macrophages. *Eur. J. Pharmacol.* **367**: 379–388.
40. Hong, J, Smith, TJ, Ho, CT, August, DA and Yang CS (2001). Effects of purified green and black tea polyphenols on cyclooxygenases-and lipoxygenases-dependent metabolism of arachidonic acid in human colon mucosa and colon tumor tissues. *Biochem. Pharmacol.* **62**: 1175–1183.
41. Aucamp, J, Gaspar, A, Hara, Y and Apostolides, Z (1997). Inhibition of xanthine oxidase by catechins from tea (*Camellia sinensis*). *Anticancer Res.* **17**: 4381–4385.
42. Lin, JK, Chen, PC, Ho, CT and Lin-Shiau SY (2000). Inhibition of xanthine oxidase and suppression of intracellular reactive oxygen species in HL-60 cells by

theaflavins-3,3'–digallate, (-)-epigallocatechin-3-gallate, and propyl gallate. *J. Agric. Food Chem.* **48**: 2736–2743.
43. Parkinson, A (1996). Biotransformation of xenobiotics. In: *Cassarett and Doull's Toxicology: The Basic Science of Poisons*, 5th ed., 113–186. McGraw-Hill, New York.
44. Yu, R, Jiao, JJ, Duh, JL, Gudehithlu, K, Tan, TH and Kong, AN (1997). Activation of mitogen-activated protein kinases by green tea polyphenols: Potential signalling pathways in the regulation of antioxidant-responsive element mediated phase II enzyme gene expression. *Carcinogenesis* **18**: 451–456.
45. Chen, C, Yu, R, Owuor, ED and Kong, AN (2000). Activation of antioxidant-response element (ARE), mitogen-activated protein kinases (MAPKs) and caspases by major green tea polyphenol components during cell survival and death. *Arch. Pharm. Res.* **23**: 605–612.
46. Lin, Y–L., Cheng, C–Y., Lin, Y–P., Lau, Y–W., Juan, I–M and Lin, J–K (1998). Hypolipidemic effect of green tea leaves through induction of antioxidant and phase II enzymes including superoxide dismutas, catalase, and glutathione-S-transferase in rats. *J. Agric. Food Chem.* **46**: 1893–1899.
47. Khan, SG, Katiyar, SK, Agarwal, R and Mukhtar, H (1992). Enhancement of antioxidant and phase II enzymes by oral feeding of green tea polyphenols in drinking water to SKH-1 hairless mice: possible role in cancer chemoprevention. *Cancer Res.* **52**: 4050–4052.
48. Cao, G, Sofic, E and Prior, R (1996). Antioxidant capacity of tea and common vegetables. *J. Agric. Food Chem.* **44**: 3426–3431.
49. Negishi, H, Xu, J–W, Ikeda, K, Njelekela, M and Nara, Y (2004). Black and green tea polyphenols attenuate blood pressure increases in stroke-prone spontaneously hypertensive rats. *J. Nutr.* **134**: 38–42.
50. Hodgson, JM, Puddey, IB, Croft, KD, Burke, V, Mori, TA Caccetta, RA and Beilin, LG (2000). Acute effects of ingestion of black and green tea on lipoprotein oxidation. *Am. J. Clin. Nutr.* **71**: 1103–1107.
51. Serafini, M, Ghiselli, A and Ferro-Luzzi, A (1996). *In vivo* antioxidant effect of green and black tea in man. *Eur. J. Clin. Nutr.* **50**: 28–32.

52. Maxwell, S and Thorpe, G (1996). Tea flavonoids have little short term impact on serum antioxidant activity. *Br. Med. J.* **313**: 229.
53. Van Het Hof, KH, De Boer, HS, Wiseman, SA, Lien, N, Westrate, JA and Tijburg, LB (1997). Consumption of green or black tea does not increase resistance of low-density lipoprotein to oxidation in humans. *Am. J. Clin. Nutr.* **66**: 1125–1132.
54. McAnlis, GT, McEneny, J, Pearce, J and Young, IS (1998). Black tea consumption does not protect low density lipoprotein from oxidative modification. *Eur. J. Clin. Nutr.* **52**: 202–206.
55. Benzie, IF and Strain, JJ (1999). Ferric reducing/ antioxidant power assay: Direct measure of total antioxidant activity of biological fluids and modified version for simultaneous measurement of total antioxidant power and ascorbic acid concentration. *Methods Enzymol.* **299**: 15–27.
56. Leenen, R, Rodenberg, AJ, Tijburg, LB and Wiseman, SA (2000). A single dose of tea with or without milk increases plasma antioxidant activities in humans. *Eur. J. Clin. Nutr.* **54**: 87–92.
57. Sung, H, Nah, J, Chun, S, Park, H, Yang, SE and Min, WK (2000). *In vivo* antioxidant effect of green tea. *Eur. J. Clin. Nutr.* **54**: 527–529.
58. Langley-Evans, S. 2000. Consumption of black tea elicits an increase in plasma antioxidant potential in humans. *Int. J. Food Sci. Nutr.* **51**: 309–315.
59. Duffy, SJ, Keaney, JF, Jr, Holbrook, M, Gokce, N, Swerdloff, PL, Frei, B and Vita, JA (2001). Short and long term black tea consumption reverses endothelial dysfunction in patients with coronary artery disease. *Circulation* **104**: 151–156.
60. Bell, C (2000). Tea for two thousand. *Souvenir of India Int. Millennium Tea Convention.* 22–24 March, 2000, New Delhi, 1–5.

Chapter 4

Dietary Flavonoids and Bioavailability

Introduction

Flavonoids have been known as plant pigments for over a century. The first observation regarding their biological activities was published in 1936[1]. Originally proposed to function as vitamins, the term 'Vitamin P' was suggested for flavonoids, although this was later dismissed[2]. Flavonoids belong to a vast group of polyphenolic compounds that are widely distributed in all foods of plant origin. Polyphenols are involved in plant growth and reproduction, provide resistance from pathogens and predators, and protect crops from disease and preharvest seed germination[3]. Now–a–days interest in the possible health benefits of polyphenols, particularly flavonoids, has increased owing to their antioxidant and free-radical scavenging abilities observed *in vitro*.

An overview of the hypothetical links between the working mechanisms and clinical effects of flavonoids is given in Fig. 4.1.

Structure

Polyphenols can be divided into at least 10 different classes based upon their chemical structure[3].

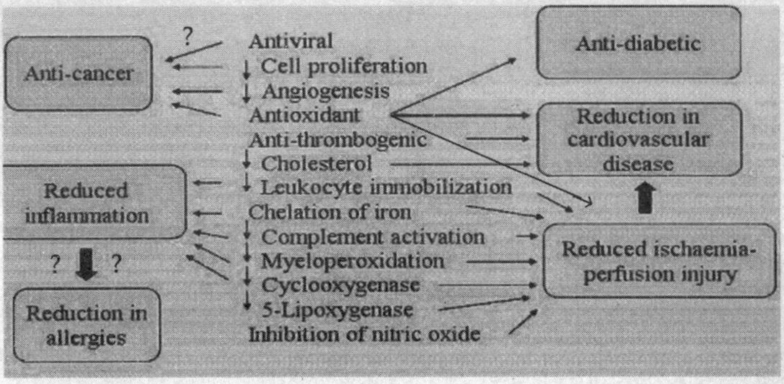

Source: Modified from Ref. 4

Fig. 4.1: Hypothesis of the links between the working mechanisms of flavonoids and their effects on disease

Polyphenols are characterised as containing two or more aromatic rings, each bearing at least one aromatic hydroxyl and connected with a carbon bridge[5]. In case of flavonoids, the largest class of polyphenols, this bridge consists of two aromatic rings linked through three carbons (Fig. 4.2). Biogenetically, the A ring usually arises from a molecule of resorcinol or phloroglucinol synthesised from the acetate pathway and has a characteristic hydroxylation pattern at the 5 and 7 position[6]. The B ring comes from the shikimate pathway and is usually 4′–, 3′4′–, or 3′4′5′–hydroxylated. Further, based upon variations in the heterocyclic C–ring, flavonoids can be subdivided into six major subclasses. These are: flavones, flavonols, flavanones, catechins, anthocyanidins, and isoflavones[7] (Fig. 4.3). More than 5000 subclasses of flavonoids were identified in 1990[8].

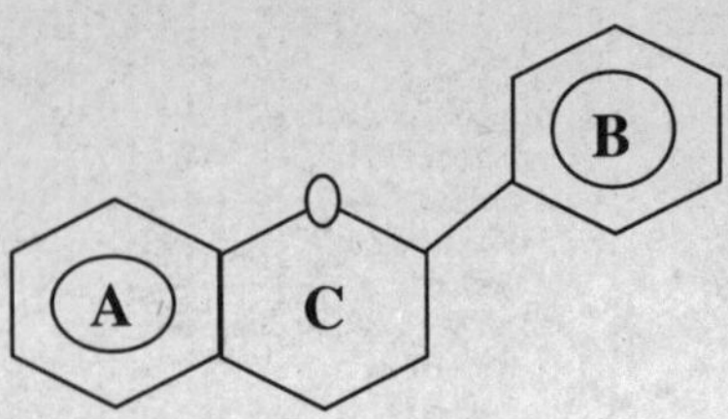

Fig. 4.2: Basic flavonoid structure

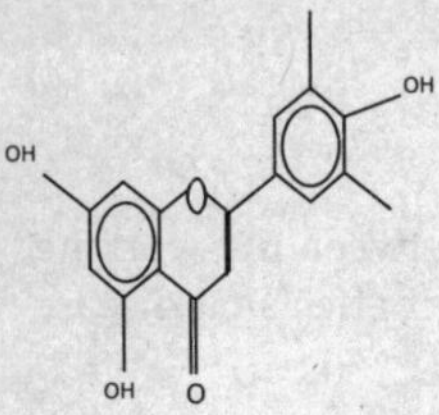

Flavones (e.g., apigenin, luteolin, diosmetin) Major food sources: Parsley, thyme, celery, sweet red pepper

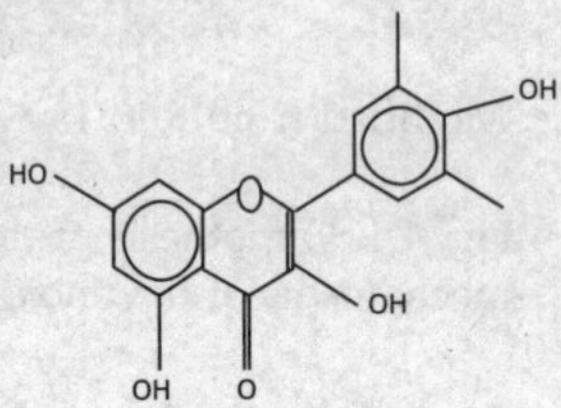

Flavonols (e.g., quercetin, myricetin, kaempferol) Major food sources: Onion, kale, broccoli, apple

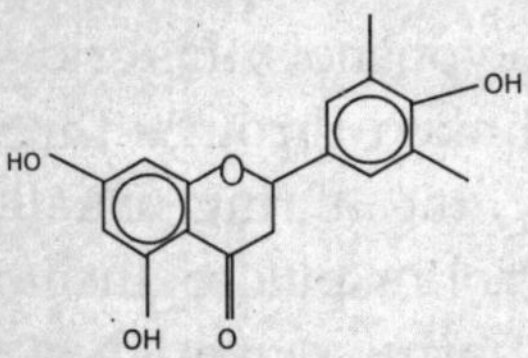

Flavanones (e.g., naringenin, hesperetin, narigin, taxifolin) Major food sources: Citrus fruits, citrus peel

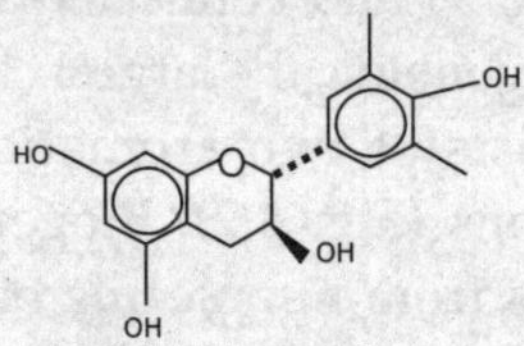

Catechins (Flavanols)
(e.g., epicatechin, gallocatechin)
Major food sources: Tea, red wine, apples, cocoa

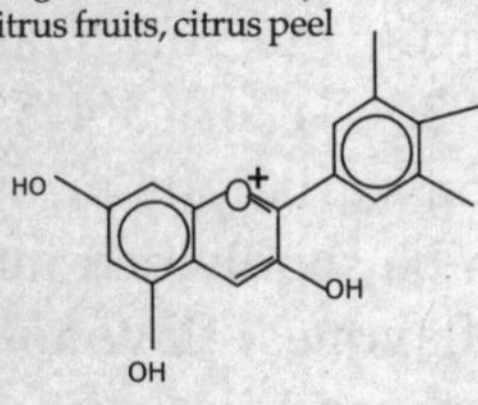

Anthocyanidins (e.g., pelargodin, malvidin, cyandin, delphinidin). Major food sources: Cherries, berries, grapes, tea, red wine, strawberries, fruit peels with dark pigments

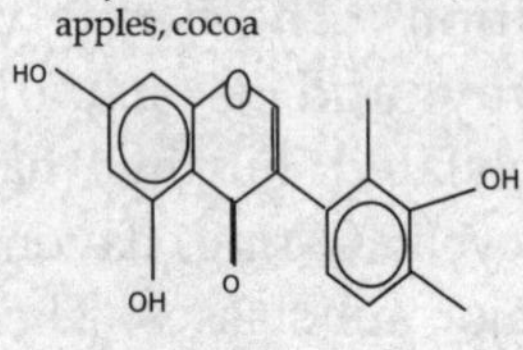

Isoflavones (e.g., genistein, daidzein) Major food sources: Soya bean, legumes

Fig. 4.3: Major subclasses of flanonoids, the individual compounds, and their food sources

Source: Ref. 7

Food Sources

Flavonoids are found in fruits, vegetables, grains, bark, roots, stems, flowers, tea, and wine. Tea and onions are the main dietary sources of flavones and flavonols. A large body of literature exists regarding their content in various foods.

A typical tea beverage contains 2500 to 3500 ppm solids[9]. Black and green tea beverages have different polyphenol constituents due to the changes that occur during manufacturing (Table 4.1).

Table. 4.1
Principal components of green and black tea beverages (% wt/wt solids)

Flavonoid	*Green Tea*	*Black Tea*
Catechins	30–42	3–10
Theaflavins	–	2–6
Simple polyphenols	2	3
Flavonols	2	1
Other polyphenols	6	23
Theanine	3	3
Amino acids	3	3
Peptides/protein	6	6
Organic acids	2	2
Sugars	7	7
Other carbohydrates	4	4
Caffeine	3–6	3–6
Potassium	5	5
Other minerals/ash	5–8	5–8

Source: Adapted from Refs. 10–12.

Bioavailability

A good understanding of the bioavailability of the active components of tea is important for knowing the biological activities and the mechanisms of action of tea *in vivo*. Early studies on the bioavailability and metabolism of tea polyphenols have been reviewed.[13, 14] Uptake of tea flavonoids is most efficient for the monomeric catechins found in green tea and in low amounts in black tea. The uptake kinetics of catechins was studied recently in humans[15]. At the time of breakfast, 1.5 mmol of ECG, EGC or EGCG was ingested by 10 healthy volunteers. Plasma and 24-h urine were analysed for catechin levels. The differences in the kinetics of appearance of the three catechins in the blood were observed. ECG was slowest to rise with a peak at 4 h and showed the slowest decline with half-life time ($t_{1/2}$) of almost 7 h. EGCG was found intermediate with a peak at 2.9 h and decline with a $t_{1/2}$ of almost 4 h. The uptake of EGC was very fast with a peak at 1.4 h and decline with a $t_{1/2}$ of 1.7 h. The maximum concentrations were 5.0 ± 0.32, 1.3 ± 0.23 and 3.1 ± 0.35 μmol/L for EGC, EGCG and ECG, respectively. Up to 13.6 per cent of the ingested EGC was excreted in the urine and a part of it was methylated. ECG and EGCG were not detected in urine.

The uptake of TF was studied [16] in two healthy volunteers after ingestion of 700 mg. It was observed that a maximum concentration of 1 μmol/L was reached after 2 h. A peak of 4.2μmol/L was found in the TF level of urine. Both plasma and urine levels were relatively low in comparison with monomeric catechins. The uptake of TF may be underestimated since the method will not detect TF metabolites with modifications in A- and C-ring.[17] The absorption of TR remains to be studied. Unabsorbed flavonoids and those excreted via bile into small intestine are degraded by bacteria in the colon. Deconjugation and ring fission of the aglycones to phenolic acids are considered the major bacterial reaction[13].

In humans, the absorption of dietary quercetin was analysed and estimated to range from 20 to 50 per cent depending on the nature of the glycoside chain.[18] It was observed that the presence of a glucose moiety enhances absorption and allows absorption as intact molecules. De Vries and coworkers conducted a feeding study [19] in which black tea (49 mg quercetin and 27 mg kaempferol) or fried onions (13 mg of quercetin and no kaempferol) were provided to 15 healthy individuals. It was reported that quercetin was readily absorbed, but absorption of quercetin from tea was half that of onions. In another randomised cross-over feeding study[20], the bioavalability of quercetin from red wine, fried onions and black tea was explored. Although some of the available flavonols from red wine were absorbed and present in plasma, the levels were lower than those found with onion as the flavonol source. The urinary excretion of quercetin was higher with red wine than with tea. It was suggested that because one glass of red wine contains fewer flavonols than either a cup of tea or one portion of fried onions, red wine is a proper source of flavonols.

The major tea catechins are predominantly (>80 per cent) found as conjugates in plasma and urine [21, 22] and these conjugates still contain intact catechol and gallate moieties. They have been shown to scavenge superoxide with the same efficacy as their parent compounds[23]. Metabolism of flavonoids takes place principally in the colon and liver [24, 25] and their transformation in the liver includes glucuronidation and sulfation of the phenolic hydroxyl groups and O-methylation of the catechol groups. Flavonoids not absorbed in the intestine or conjugates bile-excreted into the intestine are degraded by bacteria in the colon whereas hydrolysis of conjugates and glycosides and ring fission of the aglycones to phenolic acids take place as major bacterial conversions, followed by (re) absorption[25].

The study of flavonoids is complex because of the heterogeneity of the different molecular structures and the scarcity of data on the bioavailability. In order to fully understand the bioavailability of tea flavonoids,

Some Commercial Tea Products

In addition to tea as a beverage, wider applications of tea and its components are being developed. Tea's antioxidative, antibacterial, deodorant and other properties are being put to use in various fields such as the beverage market, dietetics and daily life implementation.

1. ***Catechin 100**: Polyphenon 70S is produced in a capsular form (100 mg of catechins capsule) in Japan. This is taken orally to prevent viral and bacterial and other infections. Similar type tea catechins are also sold in the US health care market.*
2. ***Catechin ACE**: This capsule contains 50 mg of tea catechins, 10 mg Gingko biloba extract, 200 I.U. of vitamin A, 20 mg and 10 mg of vitamin C and E respectively. This is being used in Japan for enhancing antioxidativity, and for those who are under oxidative stress and prone to vascular disorder.*

3. ***Catechin 100 Plus Oligo**: One tablet contains 50 mg of tea catechins and 40 mg of galacto-oligosaccharide. Intake of 6–8 tablets daily is recommended. It inhibits the growth of putrefactive bacteria and increases the growth of bifidobacteria or lactobacillus bacteria. It improves the condition of bowel.*
4. ***Bottle Health Drinks (β Catechin)**: Herbal extracts are mixed with tea catechins and β carotene to enhance the scavenging action against oxygen radicals.*
5. ***Antiflu mask**: For protection from contamination by airborne viruses, a small piece of catechin filter is fitted in a facial mask. This mask is being used mainly for protection against attack of influenza virus.*
6. ***Cosmetics**: Antioxidative potency and UV protecting functions of tea polyphenols are utilised in manufacturing different cosmetics.*
7. ***Catechin 'Macha'**: 'Macha' is mixed with polyphenon and powdered milk to make the taste less pungent.*
8. ***Catechin Enriched Soft Drink**: It is a mixture of tea catechins and other natural ingredients. This is available in 500 ml bottle.*
9. ***Catechin Candy and Chewing Gum:** These are sold in the confectionery market as dental care candy and tooth deodorants.*
10. ***Catechin Soap, Mouth Deodorising Tablets***
11. ***Theanine, Tea powder, Tea flake, Tea polysaccaride, tea saponin, Tea oil, Tea food, etc.***

Source: 1–10: Ref. 35

Box 4.1

further human studies that focus on the identification and quantification of metabolites in body fluids, and if feasible, tissues, are warranted. Besides, sensitive and selective analytical methods particularly for black tea flavonoids have to be developed.

Effect of Addition of Milk to Tea

Tea flavonoids can bind easily to proteins, and there have been suggestions that adding milk to tea will promote binding of the tea flavonoids to proteins present in the milk thereby inhibiting their uptake into the body[26]. However, a number of studies directly measuring the concentrations of flavonoids in blood after consumption of tea with or without milk suggest that this is not the case—certainly not for the simple flavonoids such as catechins and quercetin.[27] It is not yet technically possible to measure the levels of thearubigins in blood, so it is not certain what the effect of milk may be on the uptake of this major black tea flavonoid fraction. It has been reported in one study that addition of milk to black tea does not affect the increases in plasma antioxidant activity (PAA)[28]. This suggests that milk protein binding is not affecting absorption of any of the black tea flavonoid fractions[26]. In a recent study conducted with eighteen healthy volunteers, each consumed two out of four supplements, viz. black tea, black tea with milk, green tea and water. It was found that flavonols are absorbed from tea, and their bioavailability is not affected by addition of milk[29]. In another study, it was also confirmed that addition of milk to black tea does not affect the bioavailability of catechins [30]. In animal models also, few studies have examined the effects of addition of milk to tea. Although at least two studies with animal models found that adding milk to black tea did not diminish its inhibitory effect on tumorigenesis induced by chemical carcinogens[31, 32], it is unknown whether these effects were related to the antioxidant activity of tea polyphenols. However, if flavonoids from tea have beneficial effects, such effects will not be obviated by addition of milk to tea. Rather, calcium, minerals and vitamins in milk add to the benefits. Table 4.2 lists the

Table 4.2
Nutritional Value of 3 cups of tea and the milk present in 3 cups of tea (http://www.teahealth.co.uk)

Nutrient[33]	*Amount provided by 3 cups of tea alone**	*Percentage of daily recommended nutrient intake provided by tea alone****	*Amount provided by the semi-skimmed milk present in 3 cups of tea***	*Percentage of daily recommended nutrient intake provided by the milk alone in 3 cups of tea ****	*Total amount provided by 3 cups of tea* with semi-skimmed milk*
Minerals:					
Calcium	–	–	108 mg	15%	108 mg
Zinc	–	–	0.36 mg	5% (females), 4% (males)	0.36 mg
Potassium	97 mg	3%	135 mg	4%	232 mg
Manganese	0.8 mg	–	–	–	0.8 mg
Vitamins:					
Thiamine (B1)	–	–	36 mcg	5% (females), 4% (males)	36 mcg
Riboflavin	57 mcg	5% (females), 4% (males)	162 mcg	15 % (females), 13% (males)	219 mcg
Vitamin B6	–	–	54 mcg	5% (females) 4% (males)	54 mcg
Folate	–	–	5.4 mcg	3%	5.4 mcg
Niacin	0.57 mg	4% (females) 3% (males)	0.09 mg	1 % (females), 1% (males)	0.66 mg
Pantothenate		–	0.3 mg	–	0.3 mg
Vitamin B12		–	0.36 mcg	24%	0.36 mcg

Notes: *1 cup of milked tea contains 190 ml tea[34]
**Portion of milk in 1 cup = 30 ml[34]
***Based on recommended intake for 19–50 year olds.

nutrients present in 3 cups of tea, as also the nutrients present in semi-skimmed milk added to 3 cups of tea, as well as their overall contribution to recommended daily intakes and their main functions.

References

1. Rusznyak, SP and Szent-Gyorgyi, A (1936). Vitamin P: flavonols as vitamins. *Nature* **138**: 27.
2. Kuo, SM (1997). Dietary flavonoid and cancer prevention: evidence and potential mechanism. *Crit. Rev. Oncogen* **8**: 47–69.
3. Bravo, LB (1998). Polyphenols: chemistry, dietary sources, metabolism, and nutritional significance. *Nutr. Rev.* **56**: 317–333.
4. Nijveldt, RJ, Nood, EV, van Hoorn, DEC, Boelens, PG, Norren, KV and van Leeuwen, PAM (2001). Flavonoids: a review of probable mechanisms of action and potential applications. *Am. J. Clin. Nutr.* **74**: 418-425.
5. Clifford, M (2001). A nomenclature for phenols with special reference to tea. *Crit. Rev. Food Sci.* Nutr. **41**(Suppl.): 393–397.
6. Croft, KD (1998). The chemistry and biological effects of flavonoids and phenolic acids. *Ann. NY Acad. Sci.* **854**: 435–442.
7. Ross, JA and Kasum, CM (2002). Dietary flavonoids: bioavailability, metabolic effects, and safety. *Annu. Rev. Nutr.* **22**: 19–34.
8. Harbourne, JB (1993). *The Flavonoids: Advances in Research since 1986*. Chapman & Hall, London.
9. Balentine, DA, Wiseman, SA and Bouwens, LCM (1997). The chemistry of tea flavonoids. *Crit. Rev. Food Sci. Nutr.* **37**: 693–704.
10. Balentine, DA (1997). Tea. In: *Kirk-Othmer Encyclopedia of Chemical Technology*. 4th ed., 747–768. John Wiley & Sons, New York.
11. Harbowy, M and Baletine, DA (1997). Tea chemistry. *Crit. Rev. Plant Sci.* **16**: 415–480.
12. Sanderson, GW (1972). The chemistry of and tea manufacturing. In: *Structural and Functional Aspects of*

Phytochemistry, Recent Advances in Phytochemistry. 247–316. eds. Runeckles, VC and Tso, TC, Academic Press, New York.

13. Hollman, PCH, Tijburg, LBM and Yang, CS (1997). Bioavailability of flavonoids from tea. *Crit. Rev. Food Sci. Nutr.* **37**: 719–738.
14. Wiseman, SA, Mulder, T and Rietveld, A (2001). Tea flavonoids: bioavailability *in vivo* and effects on cell signaling pathways *in vitro Antioxidants & Redox Signaling* **3**: 1009–1021.
15. Van Amelsvoort, JM, Van Hof, KH, Mathot, JN, Mulder, TP, Wiersma, A. and Tijburg, LB 2001. Plasma concentrations of individual tea catechins after a single oral dose in humans. *Xenobiotica* **31**: 891–901.
16. Rietveld, A. and Wiseman, S (2003). Antioxidant effects of tea: evidence from human clinical trials. *J. Nutr.* **133**: 3285S–3292S.
17. Mulder, TP, Van Platerink, CJ, Wijnand Schuyl, PJ and Van Amelsvoort, JM (2001). Analysis of theaflavins in biological fluids using liquid chromatography-electrospray mass spectrometry. *J. Chromatogr. B. Biomed. Sci. Appl.* **760**: 271–279.
18. Hollman, PCH, De Vries, JHM, Van Leeuwen, SD, Mengelers, MJB and Katan, MB 1995. Absorption of dietary quercetin glycosides and quercetin in healthy ileostomy volunteers. *Am. J. Clin. Nutr.* **62**: 1276–1282.
19. De Vries, JHM, Hallman, PCH, Meyboom, S., Buysman, MNCP, Zock, PL, van Staveren, WA. and Katan, MB 1998. Plasma concentrations and urinary excretion of the antioxidant flavonols quercetin and kaempferol as biomarkers for dietary intake. *Am. J. Clin. Nutr.* **68**: 60–65.
20. De Vries, JHM, Hallman, PCH, van Amersfoort, I, Olthof, MR and Katan, MD 2001. Red wine is a poor source of bioavailable flavonols in men. *J. Nutr.* **131**: 745–748
21. Lee, MJ, Wang, ZY, Li, H, Chen, L, Sun, Y, Gobbo, S, Balentine, DA and Yang CS 1995. Analysis of plasma and urinary tea polyphenols in human subjects. *Cancer Epidemiol. Biomarkers Prev.* **4**: 393–399.
22. Rice-Evans, CA., Miller, NJ and Paganga, G (1996). Structure-antioxidant activity relationships of flavonoids and phenolic acids. *Free Radic. Biol. Med.* **20**: 933–956.

23. Harada, M, Kan, Y, Naoki, H, Fukui, Y, Kageyama, N, Nakai, M, Miki, W and Kiso, Y 1999. Identification of the antioxidative metabolides in biological fluids of the rat with ingested (+)–catechin and (–)–epicatechin. *Biosci. Biotechnol. Biochem.* **63**: 973–977.
24. Das, NP (1971). Studies on flavonoid metabolism. Absorption and metabolism of (+)–catechin in man. *Biochem. Pharmacol.* **20**: 3435–3445.
25. Shaw, IC and Griffiths, LA (1980). Identification of the major biliary metabolites of (+)-catechin in the rat. *Xenobiotica* **10**: 905–911.
26. Wiseman, SA (2002). Tea, health and getting the message across. *Planters Chronicle* **98**: 17–18.
27. Van Het Hof, KH, Kivits, GAA, Weststrate, JA and Tijburg, LBM 1998. Bioavailability of catechins from tea: the effect of milk. *Eur. J. Clin. Nutr.* **52**: 356–359.
28. Leenen, R, Roodenburg, AJC., Tijburg, LBM and Wiseman, SA 2000. A single dose of tea with or without milk increases plasma antioxidant activity in humans. *Eur. J. Clin. Nutr.* **54**: 87–92.
29. Hollman, PCH, van het Hof, KH, Tijburg, LBM and Katan, MB 2001. Addition of milk does not affect the absorption of flavonols from tea in man. *Free Rad.Res.* **34**: 297–300.
30. Van Het Hof, KH, Wiseman, SA, Yang, CS and Tijburg, LBM (1999). Plasma and lipoprotein levels of tea catechins following repeated tea consumption. *Proc. Soc. Exp. Biology Med.* **220**: 203-209.
31. Record, IR and Dreosti, IE 1998. Protection by tea against UV–A + B-induced skin cancers in hairless mice. *Nutr. Cancer* **32**: 71–75.
32. Weisburger, JH, Rivenson, A. Garr, K and Aliaga, C (1997). Tea, or tea and milk, inhibit mammary gland and colon carcinogenesis in rats. *Cancer Lett.* **114**: 323–327.
33. Holland, B, Welch, AA, Unwin, I.D, Buss, DH, Paul, AA and Southgate, DAT. *The Composition of Foods.* 5th edition, Royal Society of Chemistry, Cambridge.
34. Crawley, H (1988). Food portion sizes. MAFF.
35. Hara, Y (2001). *Green Tea: Health Benefits and Applications.* Marcel Dekker Inc., New York, p. 252.

Chapter 5

Prevention of Cardiovascular Disease

Coronary Heart Disease

The onset of cardiovascular disease (CVD) depends on numerous factors that can be modulated by components in the diet. Hertog and colleagues[1] examined the relation between CVD and flavonoid consumption (tea, apples, onions) in 805 elderly men (the Zutphen Study). This prospective cohort study demonstrated a marked reduction in cardiovascular risk in the tertile of subjects with the highest flavonoid consumption compared with individuals with lowest consumption. Specifically, they observed that individuals consuming >29 mg/day had a 68% reduction in cardiovascular risk, after adjustments for other known risk factors. Recently, Mennen and coworkers[2] observed that a high consumption of flavonoids may lower cardiovascular risk through antioxidant capacity. They had performed a cross-sectional analysis in 1286 women and 1005 men of the SU.VI.MAX Study (an 8–y trial evaluating the effect of antioxidant supplementation on the incidence of major chronic diseases). It was reported that the flavonoid-rich food consumption was inversely related to systolic blood pressure in women ($p = 0.005$). No relation between risk factors and flavonoid-rich food consumption was seen in men. Women in the highest tertile of flavonoid-rich food consumption were at lower risk of CVD (OR: 0.31; 95 per cent CI: 0.14, 0.68), whereas a positive tendency was seen in men (OR: 1.38; 95 per cent CI: 0.96, 2.00). Arts and colleagues[3] evaluated the effect of a high catechin intake by using data from the Zutphen Study and reported that catechins, whether from tea or other sources, may reduce the risk of ischemic heart disease mortality but not of stroke. Sesso and coworkers[4] in Boston Area Health Study observed that individuals who consumed one or more cups a day of tea in the previous year had a 44% lower risk of myocardial infarction (MI) than those who drank no tea. The outcome of this control study (n = 338/group) was independent of other coronary risk factors. A significant linear trend across levels of tea intake was observed ($p = 0.012$). Using a prospective cohort design, Mukamal and colleagues[5] examined the relation between tea consumption and myocardial infarction (MI). They assessed tea consumption in 1900 patients with MI in the United States for 3.8 years. This study demonstrated a 31 per cent and 39 per cent reduction in cardiovascular risk in moderate (5 cups/day) and heavy (12 cups/day) tea drinkers after adjustment for other risk factors.

Because flavonoids are thought to represent the cardioprotective components of tea, a number of investigators have re-examined the relationships between CVD and tea consumption in cohort studies (Table 5.1). The sources of dietary flavonoids vary between studies. It was reported in a longitudinal study[6] that an increased intake of tea and flavonoids may contribute to the primary prevention of ischemic heart disease. Conversely, in a study conducted at Caerphilly,

Wales, no association was reported in a 14 years follow-up of 334 men of 45 to 59 years of age, and a positive association with total mortality (RR: 1.4, 95% CI: 1.0–2.0, p = 0.014)[7]. However, slight positive association between increased tea consumption and coronary morbidity and all-cause mortality was reported in Scottish Heart Health Study [8] where 11,567 men and women of 49 to 59 years of age participated. Further, in a prospective study on women with a mean follow-up of 6.9 years, it was reported that flavonoid intake is not strongly associated with a reduced risk of CVD. The nonsignificant inverse associations for broccoli, apple, and tea with CVD were not mediated by flavonoids and warrant further study[9]. In a US College Alumni Health Study, black tea intake was also not found to be strongly associated with the reduced risk of CVD[10]. Recently, Vita reviewed several studies[11] that suggested no beneficial effects of flavonoids and tea consumption and discussed a number of explanations for these conflicting results. An analysis of tea consumption in relation to stroke, MI and all chronic heart disease (CHD) was based on 10 cohort and 7 case-control studies conducted by Peters and coworkers[12]. Two studies each from United Kingdom and United States indicated an increasing risk with increasing tea consumption whereas the other studies indicated a decrease in risk. The risk estimates were standardised by measuring the effects per 3 cups of tea/day. In the four studies showing an increased risk of CHD or MI and in other studies on CHD or MI, the risk decreased (RR = 0.89, 95% CI: 0.79–1.01). For stroke, one of six studies showed an increased risk of 51 per cent with each 3 cups/day, whereas the other studies indicated a decrease in risk of 26–66 per cent with each increment

Table 5.1
Some prospective cohort studies of tea and flavonoid consumption and cardiovascular disease risk

Country	*Subjects/Events (Follow-up period)*	*Outcome: Association*	*RR (95% CI)*	*Reference*
Tea				
Japan (Green Tea)	5910 non-smoking, non-drinking women, 174 cases of stroke (4 y)	Stroke incidence: Inverse	Incidence of stroke (% of cohort) 0 cups/day: 2.26% 3–4 cups/day: 0.40% ($P < 0.01$) ≥ 5 cups/day: 0.41% ($P < 0.01$)	64
Norway (Black Tea)	9856 men, 141CHD deaths; 10,233 women 18 CHD deaths (12 y)	CHD mortality: Non-significant	Men ≥ 1 cup/d vs < 1 cup/d: RR = 0.64 (0.38-1.07) Women Too few deaths to calculate RR	50
US (Black Tea)	125,356 men + women, 539 CHD deaths; 433 MI deaths; 275 stroke deaths (8 y)	CHD mortality, MI mortality, and stroke mortality: Non-significant	Risk (per cup/d) CHD mortality: RR = 0.99 (NS); MI mortality: RR = 0.97 (NS); Stroke mortality: RR = 0.94 (NS)	52
Netherlands (Black Tea)	805 men, 43 CHD deaths (5 y)	CHD mortality: Inverse	251–500 ml/d vs ≤ 250 ml/d: RR = 0.38 (0.19–0.82) >500 ml/d vs = 250 ml/d: RR= 0.45 (0.22–0.93)	1
US (Black Tea)	34,789 men, 44 CHD deaths (2 y)	CHD mortality: Non-significant	≥ 2 cups/d vs 0 cups/d: RR = 1.59 (0.98–2.28)	61
Netherlands (Black Tea)	552 men, 42 first or non-fatal stroke cases (15 y)	Stroke incidence: Inverse	Tea consumption from 1960–1970 ≥ 587 g/d vs < 330 g/d: RR = 0.31 (0.12–0.84)	65
UK/Wales (Black Tea)	1900 men, 186 IHD cases, 131 IHD deaths (14 y)	IHD incidence: Non-significant IHD mortality: Positive	IHD incidence: P (trend) = 0.67 IHD mortality: 900–1200 ml/d vs ≤ 300 ml/d: RR = 2.1 (1.0–4.1) > 1200 ml/day vs < 300 ml/d: RR = 2.3 (1.0–5.1)	8
UK/Scotland (Black Tea)	11,567 men and women 206 CHD deaths (8 y)	CHD mortality: Men: Non-significant Women: Non-significant	Men 5+ cups/d vs 0 cups/d: RR = 2.19 (NS) Women 5+ cups/d vs 0 cups/d: RR = 2.77 (NS)	8
US (Black Tea)	34,492 women 483 CHD deaths (10 y)	CHD mortality: Non-significant	5–42 times/wk vs 0 times/wk: RR = 0.89 (0.67–1.17)	62
Netherlands (Black Tea)	3454 men and women, 55% of whom had some degree of aortic atherosclerosis	Aortic atherosclerosis: Inverse	Compared to non-drinkers ≤ 250 ml/day: OR = 0.54 (0.32-0.92) 251–500 ml/day: OR = 0.47 (0.27-0.81)	24

Country	*Subjects/Events (Follow-up period)*	*Outcome: Association*	*RR (95% CI)*	*Reference*
	revealed in X–ray (2–3 y)		≥ 500 ml/day: OR = 0.31(0.16-0.59)	
Japan (Green Tea)	8522 men and women, 274 CHD deaths (13 y)	CHD mortality: Inverse for men Non-significant for women	Men ≥10 cups/d vs ≤ 3 cups/d: RR = 0.58 (0.34-0.99) Women ≥10 cups/d vs ≤ 3 cups/d: RR = 0.90 (0.60-1.37)	63
Finland (Black Tea)	26,415 male smokers, 736 cerebral infarction cases, 83 subarachnoid haemorrhage cases, 95 intracerebral haemorrhage cases (6 y)	Stroke incidence: Non-significant for all 3 subtypes	≥ 1 cup/d vs < 1 cup/d: Cerebral infarction: RR = 0.90 (0.74–1.09) Subarachnoid haemorrhage: RR = 0.71 (0.38–1.35) Intracerebral haemorrhage: RR = 0.98 (0.57–1.68)	60
Finland (Black Tea)	25,372 male smokers, 1,122 non-fatal MI, 815 CHD deaths (6 y)	Non-fatal MI incidence and CHD mortality: Non-significant	Non-fatal MI ≥1 cup (170 ml)/d vs < 1 cup/d RR= 0.94 (0.81–1.11) CHD mortality ≥ 1 cup/d vs < 1 cup/d: RR= 1.09 (0.91-1.30)	66
Flavonoids				
Finland (Flavonoids; no data on tea)	2748 men and 2385 women, 473 CHD deaths (26 y)	CHD mortality:	Men Non-significant > 4.8 mg/d vs < 2.1 mg/d: RR = 0.67 (0.44-1.00) Women >5.5 mg/d vs < 2.4 mg/d: RR =0.73 (0.41-1.32)	67
US (Flavonols and flavones)	Primary analysis: 34,789 men, 486 non-fatal MI cases (6 y)	Non-fatal MI: Non-significant	Non fatal MI 40.0 mg/d vs 7.1 mg/d: RR= 1.08 (0.81–1.43)	61
	Secondary analysis: 4814 men with prevalent CHD, 140 CHD deaths (2 y)	CHD mortality: Non-significant	CHD mortality 40.0 mg/d vs 7.1 mg/d: RR = 0.63 (0.33–1.20)	
Netherlands (Flavonoids)	552 men, 42 stroke cases (15 y)	Stroke incidence: Inverse	<18.3 mg/day: 1,00 18.3–28.5 mg/d vs < 18.3 mg/d: RR= 0.46 (0.24-0.90) ≥28.6 mg/d vs. 18.3 mg/d: RR = 0.27 (0.11-0.70) P (trend) = 0.004	65
Netherlands (Flavonoids)	804 men, 90 deaths from CHD, 92 episodes of first MI (10 y)	CHD mortality: Inverse	CHD mortality 19.1–29.9 mg/d vs ≤19 mg/d: RR = 0.58 (0.35–0.95) >29.9 mg/d vs ≤ 19 mg/d: RR = 0.47 (0.27-0.82)	68
		First MI: Non-significant	First MI > 29.9 mg/d vs ≤ 19 mg/d: RR = 0.62: (0.24–1.05)	
UK/Wales (Flavonols)	1900 men, 186 1HD cases, 131 IHD deaths (14 y)	IHD incidence: Non-significant	IHD incidence > 34 mg/d vs < 19 mg/d: RR=1.1 (0.6–1.6)	7
		IHD mortality:	IHD mortality	

Country	*Subjects/Events (Follow-up period)*	*Outcome: Association*	*RR (95% Cl)*	*Reference*
		Non-significant	> 34 mg/d vs < 19 mg/d: RR=1.6 (0.9-2.9)	
Finland (Flavones and flavonols)	26,415 male smokers, 736 cerebral infarctions, 83 subarachnoid haemorrhages 95 intracerebral haemorrhages (6 y)	Stroke incidence: Non-significant for all 3 subtypes	16.4 mg/d vs 4.2 mg/d: Cerebral infarction RR = 0.98 (0.80–1.21) Subarachnoid haemorrhage RR = 0.75 (0.40–1.41) Intracerebral hemorrhage: RR = 0.88 (0.59-1.57)	60
Finland (Flavones and flavonols)	25,372 male smokers, 1122 non-fatal MI, 815 CHD deaths (6 y)	Non-fatal MI: Inverse	Non-fatal MI 10.8 mg/d vs 3.9 mg/d: RR = 0.77 (0.64–0.93) 17.8 mg/d vs 3.9 mg/d: RR = 0.77 (0.64–0.93)	66
		CHD mortality: Non-significant	CHD mortality 17.8 mg/d vs 3.9 mg/d: RR = 0.89 (0.71–1.11)	
Netherlands (Catechins)	806 men, 90 deaths from CHD, 90 cases of MI, 47 deaths from stroke 88 cases of stroke (10 y)	CHD mortality: Inverse	CHD mortality 86-355 mg/d vs ≤ 49 mg/d: RR = 0.49 (0.27–0.88)	3
		MI incidence: Non-significant	MI incidence: 86–355 mg/d vs ≤ 49 mg/d: RR = 0.70 (0.39–1.59)	
		Stroke mortality: Non-significant	Stroke mortality: 86-355 mg/d vs ≤ 49 mg/d: RR = 0.81 (0.36–1.83)	
		Stroke incidence: Non-significant	Stroke incidence 86-355 mg/d vs ≤ 49 mg/d: RR = 0.92 (0.51–1.68)	

of 3 cups/day. European, for example, tends to drink stronger tea than a North American, therefore, the effect per cup of tea could be higher in the European studies. In fact, there are lots of challenges to the investigators in conducting clinical trials with tea. For example, not only are the kind of tea and their preparation important, but the frequency and timings of intake are also critical factors because they affect the pharmacokinetics and ultimate disposition of the polyphenols within tissues[13]. This apart, interindividual variations in the bioavailability of the tea polyphenols can be substantial and may be due in part to differences in colonic microflora and genetic polymorphisims among the enzymes involved in polyphenol metabolism[14]. The effect of tea drinking may also differ by genotype, e.g., individuals with E2 allele of ApoE possess a reduced plasminogen activator inhibitor (PAI 1) activity following consumption of black tea[15]. Recently, Menon and colleagues evaluated[16] the relationship of tea consumption with cardiovascular risk factors in 2,926 participants in France. It was observed, waist-hip ratio, total cholesterol, serum-triglycerides and fasting glucose decreased with increasing tea consumption in women, whereas BMI (body mass index), blood pressure, and serum-triglycerides were related with tea consumption in men (*p* for trend between 0.002 and 0.05). Fruit and vegetable consumption increased, and consumption of meat and coffee decreased with increasing tea consumption (*p* for trend ranged from 0.0001 to 0.04). Total fat intake was found positively related to tea consumption (*p* for trend = 0.0005 in men and 0.0001 in women). They advocated the importance of lifestyle factors in future studies. Another National Cross-sectional Study of 3,430 men and women aged 30–70 years conducted in Saudi Arabia showed a significant inverse relationship between tea drinking and blood lipid levels. There was also a positive dose-response effect between tea consumption and CHD that was persistent after adjustment for various risk factors. It was also indicated that people who drank more than 6 cups of black tea (>480 ml) per day had a significantly lower prevalence of CHD than the non–tea drinkers[17].

There is accumulating evidence that postprandial lipaemia makes a substantial contribution to the incidence of CHD. Recently, Unno and coworkers evaluated[17a] the effect of tea catechins on the postprandial response of plasma triacylglycerols after an oral fat load on human subjects. In a randomized triple-crossover design, nine male subjects with mild or borderline hypertriacylglycerolaemia consumed 10 (control), 224 (moderate dose) and 674 mg (high dose) of the assigned tea catechins three times each along with a standardized light meal consisting of a piece of bread spread with 20 g butter. Plasma lipids were measured in the fasting state and 1, 2, 3, 4 and 6 h after consuming the light meal. It was observed that, compared with the control, moderate and high doses of tea catechins reduced the incremental area under the plasma triacylglycerol curves by 15.1 and 28.7 per cent respectively. Next, the rapid evaluation of remnant-like particle cholesterol was significantly inhibited by a high dose of tea catechins 2 h after consuming the light meal ($p<0.01$). In the range of tea catechin dosages, no significant differences were observed in the postprandial responses for plasma total cholesterol or NEFA at any time point. Unno and coworkers concluded that tea catechins attenuated the postprandial increase in plasma triacylglycerol levels following a fat load.

However, according to Mckay and Blumberg, not taking into account socioeconomic and lifestyle factors in these studies as well as the inadequate methodology used to define tea preparation and intake were responsible for obtaining conflicting results by various human studies[18]. These factors are thus important, and in future studies on the relationship between tea consumption and CHD, possible confounding by lifestyle and other factors stated above has to be taken into account.

Atherosclerosis

Atherosclerosis is considered a disease with a strong inflammatory component. The possible mechanisms of the anti-inflammatory action of flavonoids have been reviewed[19]. Tea polyphenols may prevent development of atherosclerosis and other CVDs by protecting low-density lipoproteins (LDL) against oxidation[20] as shown *in vitro*[21] but not convincingly demonstrated *in vivo*[22] though it has been showed [23] in a controlled intervention that black tea can inhibit *ex vivo* lipoprotein oxidation acutely. In the prospective Rotterdam Study of 3,454 adults, 55 years of age or older, followed for two to three years, Geleijnse and colleagues examined aortic atherosclerosis via x–ray measurement of calcified deposits in the abnormal aorta[24]. The odds ratio (OR) for drinking 125–250 mL (1–2 cups) of tea daily was 0.54 (95 per cent CI: 0.32–0.92) and decreased to 0.31 (95 per cent CI: 0.16–0.59) when > 500 mL/day (more than four cups) were consumed. In Japan, atherosclerosis by coronary arteriography was determined in 512 patients over 30 years of age and reported a protective effect of tea among those (262 men) not being treated for diabetes was reported[25]. The OR of significant stenosis was 0.5 (95 per cent CI: 0.2–1.2) for those consuming 2–3 cups of green tea and 0.4 (95 per cent of CI: 0.2–0.9) for those drinking 4 or more cups/day compared to subjects consuming 1 cup or less/day.

Lipoprotein Oxidation

In order to prevent CVD it is very important to keep the cholesterol level in the blood within normal range. Tea has been shown to strengthen blood vessels and to decrease the cholesterol level in the blood stream[26, 27]. It was demonstrated that 'crude catechin' and its main component EGCG suppress an excessive rise of cholesterol concentrations[28]. The susceptibility of LDL to oxidative modification is readily inhibited *in vitro* by extracts of black and green tea[21, 29]. The effects of black tea consumption on lipid and lipoprotein concentrations in mildly hypercholesterolemic adults have been examined recently[30]. 7 men and 8 women participated in a randomised Double-Blind Cross over Study. Five servings/day of tea were compared with a caffeine free placebo beverage that tasted like tea. To assess caffeine effects, caffeine was added to the placebo in an amount equal to that in the black tea. It was observed that the five servings/day reduced total cholesterol by 6.5 per cent, LDL cholesterol by 11.1 per cent, apolipoprotein B by 5 per cent and lipoprotein (a) by 16.4 per cent compared with the placebo with added caffeine. Thus, inclusion of tea in the diet has the potential to significantly reduce blood cholesterol, thereby reducing the risk of CVD. However, *ex vivo* studies have shown little or no inhibition of LDL oxidation[21, 23, 29, 31, 32]. In a healthy cohort of 20 men, Hodgson and coworkers[22] reported a greater lag time before LDL oxidation in case of both black and green tea drinkers in comparison with water drinkers. But these changes were either on borderline (p = 0.05 for black tea) or not significant (p = 0.17 for green tea). Van het Hof[31] observed an accumulation of tea catechins in 18 healthy adults of 18 to 64 years of age, after daily consumption of 8 cups of black tea, green tea or black tea with milk for 3 days, but the concentration attained was not sufficient to enhance LDL resistance to Cu^{2+}-induced oxidation. However, Miura and colleagues [32] detected an increase in lag time (p<0.05) in 22 young men after they consumed extract of green tea (equivalent to 7 to 8 cups/ day) for seven days. The plasma β-carotene was found higher (p<0.01) in the tea group after the intervention. The difference between *in vitro* and *ex vivo* on the susceptibility of LDL to oxidation may be due to the inability to achieve concentrations *in vivo* as great as those obtained with the former methods[29].

Flavonoids like quercetin, myricetin, and kaempferol can also protect LDL from oxidation by regenerating tocopherol, an important endogenous antioxidant in humans[33].

Platelet Aggregation and Cell Adhesion Molecules

Protective effects of drinking black tea against CVDs may also involve decrease in collagen induced platelet activity[34] which might lower the risk of thrombosis[35]. Polyphenols found in black tea inhibit platelet aggregation *in vitro*[19, 36] but controlled dietary intervention studies in humans using reasonably pure preparations of polyphenolic compounds have found no significant effects on platelet aggregation.[37] In addition, it has been shown that regular ingestion of black tea for a period of four weeks does not alter platelet aggregation *ex vivo* in fasting plasma[38]. Another potential mechanism for protective effects of drinking black tea involves effects on cell adhesion molecules[38]. In the development of atherosclerosis, cellular interactions involving various cell adhesion molecules are critical[39], and may have a role in thrombogenesis[40]. Though the effects of drinking tea on adhesion molecules have not been examined but the results of several studies indicate that the polyphenols may inhibit the expression of cell adhesion molecules[41, 42].

Endothelial Cell Function (Blood Vessel Dilation)

Endothelial damage appears to be important in the development and progression of atherosclerosis and thrombogenesis[43]. Impaired vascular functions are associated with CVDs, and believed to be an early indicator of vascular diseases[44]. Protective effects of black tea against CVDs include improvements in vascular function[45, 46]. Improved vasodilator function in conduit arteries by drinking black tea has been reported in a recent Australian study[47]. In this study, tea consumption reduced plasma levels of P–selectin, a marker of *in vivo* platelet aggregation, but had no effect on other adhesion molecules. Vasodilation is mediated by nitric oxide, produced by cells lining the blood vessels. Nitric oxide inhibits the proliferation of vascular smooth muscle cells and the formation of other noncellular components that comprise the matrix of the vascular wall and, thus, is relevant to lesion formation and vascular compliance. Nitric oxide, despite affecting conduit arteries where lesions develop, also affects micro vessels that regulate flow of blood to tissues[11] Therefore, an impairment of nitric oxide formation would have adverse effects on the cardiovascular system. Endothelial function, including brachial artery flow mediated dilation, is gaining increasing acceptance as a clinically relevant surrogate endpoint for CVD risk. Although these findings cannot be interpreted as meaning that tea consumption should be recommended for the prevention or treatment of CVDs but they provide mechanistic insight and certainly suggest that tea consumption has a beneficial effect. Despite this, the American Heart Association has recommended that Americans should increase their consumption of fruits

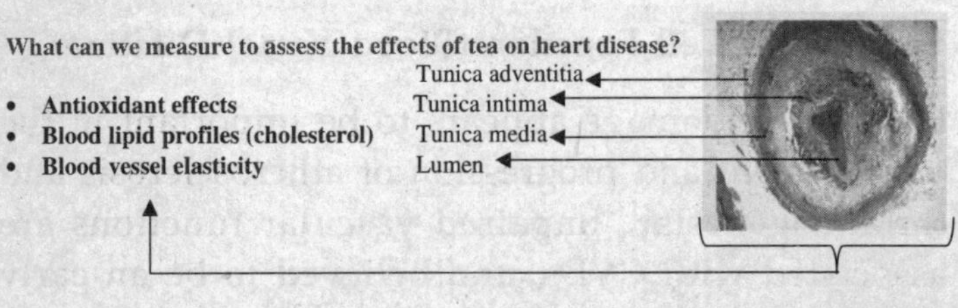

and vegetables, including a vegetable-based beverage like tea[11].

Hypertension

Sustained improvement in endothelial function could also contribute to lower blood pressure[48]. The potential effect of ingestion of tea on blood pressure has been investigated in several studies[17, 45, 47]. Investigations of the longer-term effects of regular ingestion of tea on blood pressure are limited to cross-sectional studies. Earlier cross-sectional studies reported insignificant relationships of tea intake with blood pressure. Recently, Negishi and coworkers reported that black and green tea polyphenols attenuate blood pressure increases through their antioxidant properties in Stroke-Prone Spontaneously Hypertensive Rats[49]. Inverse relationships of tea intake with blood pressure[50, 51] and the prevalence of hypertension[52] have also been reported. Conversely, in a case study, drinking black and green tea in moderate quantities did not improve blood pressure in humans[53-55]. It has been reported that theanine, in high doses, decreases significantly the blood pressure in a spontaneously hypertensive rats but does not alter blood pressure in normal rats, although it decreases the brain 5-hydroxyindole level in both types of animals[56]. This subject has not been fully investigated[57]. Hodgson and coworkers have reported that 4–OMGA (4–*O*–methylgallic acid) is a potential biomarker for black tea-derived polyphenol exposure[58]. Recently, the relationships of tea intake and a biomarker of exposure of tea-derived polyphenols (4–*O*–methylgallic acid) with blood pressure in a cross-sectional study of 218 womens (>70 years) was investigated. The observed associations for both tea intake and 4–*O*–methylgallic acid are consistent with the hypothesis that long-term regular ingestion of tea may have a favourable effect on blood pressure in older women[48].

Coronary Circulation

Epidemiological studies suggest that tea consumption decreases the risk for cardiovascular events. However, there has been no clinical report examining the effects of tea consumption on coronary flow velocity reserve (CFVR). Recently, a double-blind crossover study of 10 healthy male volunteers was conducted to compare the effects of black tea and caffeine on coronary circulation. CFVR was found to increase significantly after consumption of black tea (BT) and the ratio of BT group was greater than that of caffeine group. This study indicates that consumption of BT improves coronary vessel function as determined by CFVR[59].

References

1. Hertog, MGL, Feskens, EJM, Hollman, PCH, Katan, MB and Kromhout, D (1993). Dietary antioxidant flavonoids and the risk of coronary heart disease: the Zutphen Elderly Study. *Lancet* **342**: 1007–1011.
2. Mennen, LI, Sapinho, D, de Bree, A, Arnault, A, Bertrais, S, Galan, P and Hercberg, S (2004). Consumption of foods rich in flavonoids is related to a decreased cardiovascular risk in apparently healthy French women. *J. Nutr.* **134**: 923–926.
3. Arts, ICW, Hollman, PCH, Feskens, EJM, Mesquita, HBB and Kromhout, D (2001). Catechin intake might explain the inverse relation between tea consumption and ischemic heart disease: the Zutphen Elderly Study. *Am. J. Clin. Nutr.* **74**: 227–232.
4. Sesso, HD, Gaziano, JM, Buring, JE and Hennekens, CH (1999). Coffee and tea intake and the risk of myocardial infarction. *Am. J. Epidemiol.* **149**: 162–167.

5. Mukamal, KJ, Maclure, M, Muller, JE, Sherwood, JB and Mittleman, MA (2002). Tea consumption and mortality after acute myocardial infarction. *Circulation* **105**: 2476–2481.
6. Geleijnse, JM, Launer, LJ, Kuip van der, DAM, Hofman, A and Witteman, CM (2002). Inverse association of tea and flavonoid intakes with incident myocardial infarction: the Rotterdam study. *Am. J. Clin. Nutr.* **75**: 880-886.
7. Hertog, M, Sweetnam, P, Fehily, A, Elwood, P and Kromhout, D (1997). Antioxidant flavonols and ischemic heart disease in a Wales population in men: the Caerphilly Study *Am. J. Clin. Nutr.* **65**: 1489–1494.
8. Woodward, M and Tunstall-Pedoe, H (1999). Coffee and tea consumption in the Scottish Heart Health Study follow up: conflicting relations with coronary risk factors, coronary disease, and all cause mortality. *J. Epidemiol. Community Health* **53**: 481–487.
9. Sesso, HW, Gaziano, JM, Liu, S, and Buring, JE (2003a). Flavonoid intake and the risk of cardiovascular disease in women. *Am. J. Clin. Nutr.* **77**: 1400–1408.
10. Sesso, HD, Paffenbarger Jr, RS, Oguma, Y, and Lee, M–J (2003b) Lack of association between tea and cardiovascular disease in college alumni. *Intl. J. Epidemiol.* **32**: 527-533.
11. Vita, JA (2003). Tea consumption and cardiovascular disease: effects on endothelial function. *J. Nutr.* **133**: 3293S–3297S.
12. Peters, U, Poole, C and Arab, A. (2001). Does tea affect cardiovascular disease? A meta analysis. *Am. J .Epidemiol.* **154**: 495-503.
13. Blumberg, J (2003). Introduction to the proceedings of the third international scientific symposium on tea and human health: role of flavonoids in diet. *J. Nutr.* **133**: 3244S–3246S.
14. Scalbert, A and Williamson, G (2000). Dietary intake and bioavailability of polyphenols. *J. Nutr.* **130**: 2073S-2085S.
15. Loktionov, A, Bingham, S, Vorster, H, Jerling, J, Runswick, S, and Cummings, J (1998). Apolipoprotein E genotype modulates the effect of black tea drinking on blood lipids and blood coagulation factors: a pilot study. *Br. J Nutr.* **79**: 133–139.

16. Menon, LI, Malvy, D, Galan, P, Preziosi, P, Bertrais, S, Bruckert, E, Maurel, M, Franchisseur, C and Hercberg, S (2003). Tea consumption and cardiovascular risk in the SU.VI. MAX study: Are life-style factors important. *Nutr. Res.* **23**: 879-890.
17. Hakim, IA, Alsaif, MA, Alduwaihy, M, Al Rubeaan, K, Al-Nuaim, AR and Al-Attas, OS (2003). Tea consumption and the prevalence of coronary heart disease in Saudi adults: results from a Saudi national study. *Prev. Med.* **36**: 64-70.
17a. Unno, T, Tago, M, Suzuki, Y, Nozawa, A, Sagesaka, YM, Kakuda, T, Egawa, K and Kondo, K (2005). Effect of tea catechins on postprandial plasma lipid responses in human subjects. *Br. J. Nutr.***93**: 543-547.
18. McKay, DL and Blumberg, JB (2002). The role of tea in human health: an update. *J. Am. Coll. Nutr.* **21**: 1.13.
19. Formica, JV and Regelson, W (1995). Review of the biology of quercetin and related bioflavonoids. *Food Chem. Toxic.* **33**: 1061–1080.
20. Diaz, MN, Frei, B, Vita, JA, and Keany, JF (1997). Antioxidants and atherosclerotic heart disease. *N. Eng. J. Med.* **337**: 408–416.
21. Van het Hof, KH, De Boer H. SM, Wiseman, SA, Lien, N, Weststrate, JA and Tijburg, LBM (1997). Consumption of green or black tea does not increase resistance of low-density lipoprotein to oxidation in humans. *Am. J. Clin. Nutr.* **66**: 1125–1132.
22. Yang, CS and Landau, JM (2000). Effects of tea consumption on nutrition and health. *J. Nutr.* **130**: 2409–2412.
23. Hodgson, JM, Puddey, IB, Croft, KD, Burke, V, Mori, TA, Caccetta, RA and Beilin, L (2000). Acute effects of ingestion of black and green tea on lipoprotein oxidation. *Am. J. Clin. Nutr.* **71**: 1103–1107.
24. Geleijnse, JM, Launer, LJ, Hofman, A, Pols, HAP and Witteman, CM (1999). Tea flavonoids may protect against aortic atherosclerosis: the Rotterdam study. *Arch. Intern. Med.* **159**: 2170–2174.
25. Sasazuki, S, Kodama, H, Yoshimasu, K, Liu, Y, Washio, M, Tanaka, K, Tokunaga, S, Kono, S, Arai, H, Doi, Y,

Kawano, T, Nakagaki, O, Takada, Koyanagi, S, Hiyamuta, K, Nii, T, Shirai, K, Ideishi, M. Arakawa, K., Mohri, M and Takeshita, (A) (2000). Relation between green tea consumption and the severity of coronary atherosclerosis among Japanese men and women. *Ann. Epidemiol.* **10**: 401–408.

26. Mukhtar, H (2000). Tea in prevention of cancer, heart diseases, stroke and arthiritis. *Souvenir Intl. Millennium Tea Convention*, Session 4, 22–24 March, 2000, New Delhi, India, 1–37.
27. Weisburger, JH (2001). Tea and prevention of heart disease and cancer. *Proc. Intl. Conf. O-Cha. (tea) Culture and Science*, Session III, Oct. 5–8, 2001, Shizuoka, Japan, 90–94.
28. Muramatsu, K, Fukuyo, M and Hara, Y (1986). Effect of green tea catechins on plasma cholesterol level in cholesterol-fed rats. *J. Nutr. Sci. Vitaminol.* **32**: 613–622.
29. McAnlis, GT, McEneny, J, Pearce, J and Young, IS (1998). Black tea consumption does not protect low density lipoprotein from oxidative modification. *Eur. J. Clin. Nutr.* **52**: 202–206.
30. Davies, MJ, Judd, JT, Baer, DJ, Clevidence, BA, Paul, DR, Edwards, AJ, Wiseman, SA, Muesing, RA and Chen, SC (2003). Black tea consumption reduces total and LDL cholesterol in mildly Hypercholesterolemic adults. *J. Nutr.* **133**: 3298S–3302S.
31. Van Het Hof, KH, Wiseman, SA, Yang, CS and Tijburg, LBM (1999). Plasma and lipoprotein levels of tea catechins following repeated tea consumption. *Proc. Soc. Exp. Biology. Med.* **220**: 203–209.
32. Miura, Y, Chiba, T, Miura, S, Tomita, I, Umegaki, K, Ikeda, M and Tomita, T (2000). Green tea polyphenols (flavan 3–ols) prevent oxidative modification of low density lipoproteins: an *ex vivo* study in humans. *J. Nutr. Bichem.* **11**: 216–222.
33. Zhu, QY, Huang, Y and Chen, Z–Y (2000). Interaction between flavonoids and alpha-tocopherol in human low density lipoprotein. *J. Nutr. Biochem.* **11**: 14–21.
34. Balentine, DA (2001). The role of tea flavonoids in cardiovascular health. *Proc. Intl. Conf. O–Cha (tea) Culture and Science*, Session III, Oct. 5–8, 2001, Shizuoka, Japan, 84–89.

35. Hertog, MGL and Hollman, PC H (1996). Potential health effects of the dietary flavonol quercetin. *Eur. J. Clin. Nutr.* **50**: 63–61.
36. Neiva, TJC, Morais, L, Polack, M, Simoes, CMO and D'Amico, EA (1999). Effects of catechins on human blood platelet aggregation and lipid peroxidation. *Phytother. Res.* **13**: 597–600.
37. Janssen, K, Mensink, RP, Cox, FJ, Harryvan, JL, Hovenier, R, Hollman, PC and Katan, MB (1998). Effects of the flavonoids quercetin and apigenin on hemostasis in healthy volunteers: results from an *in vitro* and a dietary supplement study. *Am. J. Clin. Nutr.* **67**: 255-262.
38. Hodgson, JM, Puddey, IB, Mori, TA, Burke, V, Baker, R and Beilin, LJ (2001). Effects of regular ingestion of black tea on haemostasis and cell adhesion molecules in humans. *Eu. J. Clin. Nutr.* **55**: 881–886.
39. Price, DT and Loscalzo, J (1999). Cellular adhesion molecules and atherogenesis. *Am. J. Med.* **107**: 85-97.
40. Holvoet, P and Collen, D (1997). Thrombosis and atherosclerosis. *Curr. Opin. Lipidol.* **8**: 320–328.
41. Kobuchi, H, Roy, S, Sen, CK, Nguyen, HG and Packer, I (1999). Quercetin inhibits inducible ICAM-1 expression in human endothelial cells through the JNK pathway. *Am. J. Physiol.* **277**: C403–C411.
42. Rein, D, Paglieroni, TG, Wun, T, Pearson, DA, Schmitz, HH, Gosselin, R and Keen, C (2000). Cocao inhibits platelet activation and function. *Am. J. Clin. Nutr.* **72**: 30–35.
43. Zhang, X, Zhao, SP, Li, XP, Gao, M and Zhou, QC (2000). Endothelium dependent and—independent functions are impaired in patients with coronary heart disease. *Atherosclerosis* **149**: 19–24.
44. Schachinger, V, Britten, MB and Zeiher, AM (2000). Prognostic impact of coronary vasodilator dysfunction on adverse long-term outcome of coronary heart disease. *Circulation* **95**: 5–7.
45. Duffy, SJ, Keaney, JF Jr, Holbrook, M, Gokce, N, Swerdloff, PL, Frei, B and Vita, JA (2001). Short- and long-term Black tea consumption reverses endothelial dysfunction in patients with coronary artery disease. *Circulation* **104**: 151–156.

46. Tomasian, D, Keaney, JF and Vita, JA (2000). Antioxidants and the bioactivity of endothelium-derived nitric oxide. *Cardiovasc. Res.* **47**: 426–435.
47. Hodgson, JM, Puddey, IB, Burke, V and Watts, JF (2002). Regular ingestion of black tea improves brachial artery vasodilator function. *Clin. Sci.* **102**: 195–201.
48. Hodgson, JM, Devine, A, Puddey, IB, Chan, SY, Beilin, LJ and Prince, RL (2003). Tea intake is inversely related to blood pressure in older women. *J. Nutr.* **133**: 2883–2886.
49. Negishi, H, Xu, J-W, Ikeda, K, Njelekela, M, Nara, Y Yamori, Y (2004). Black and green tea polyphenols attenuate blood pressure increases in stroke-pron spontaneously hypertensive rats. *J. Nutr.* **134**: 38–42.
50. Stensvold, I, Tverdal, A, Solvoll, K and Foss, OP (1992). Tea consumption relationship to cholesterol, blood pressure and coronary and total mortality. *Prev. Med.* **21**: 546–553.
51. Hara, Y (2001). *Green Tea: Health Benefits and Applications.* Marcel Dekker Inc., New York, p. 252.
52. Klatsky, AL, Armstrong, MA and Friedman, GD (1993). Coffee, tea and mortality. *Ann. Epidemiol.* **3**: 375–338.
53. Hodgson, JM, Puddey, IB, Burke, V, Beilin, LJ and Jordan, N (1999). Effects on blood pressure of drinking green and black tea. *J. Hypertens.* **17**: 457–463.
54. Wakabayashi, K, Kono, S., Shinchi, K, Honjo, S, Todoroki, I, Sakurai, Y, Umeda, T, Imanishi, K and Yoshizawa, N (1998). Habitual coffee consumption and blood pressure: A study of self-defence officials in Japan. *Eur. J. Epidemiol.* **14**: 669–673
55. Bingham, S, Vorster, H, Jerling, J, Magee, E, Mulligan, A, Rundwick, S and Cummings, J (1997). Effect of black tea drinking on blood lipids, blood pressure and aspects of bowel habit. *Br. J. Nutr.* **78**: 41–55.
56. Yokogoshi, H, Kato, Y, Sagesaka-Mitane, Y, Takihara-Matsuura, T, Kakuda, T and Takeuchi, N (1995). Reduction effect of thenine on blood pressure and brain 5–hydroxyindoles in spontaneously hypertensive rats. *Biosci. Biotech. Biochem.* **59**: 615–618.

57. Tijburg, LBM, Mattern, T, Folts, JD, Weisgerber, UM and Kattan, MB (1997). Tea flavonoids and cardiovascular diseases: a review. *Crit. Rev. Food Sci. Nutr.* **37**: 771–785.
58. Hodgson, JM, Chan, SY, Puddey, IB, Devine, A, Wattanapenpaiboon, N, Wahlqvist, Ml, Lukito, W, Burke, V, Ward, NC and Croft, KD (2004). Phenolic acid metabolites as biomarkers for tea-and coffee derived polyphenol exposure in human subjects. *British J. Nutr.* **91**: 301–306.
59. Hirata, K, Shimada, K, Watanabe, H, Otsuka, R, Tokai, K, Yoshiyama, M, Homma, S and Yoshikawa, J (2004). Black tea increases coronary flow velocity reserve in healthy male subjects. *Am. J. Cardiol.* **93**: 1384–1388.
60. Hirvonen, T, Virtamo, J, Korhonen, P, Albanes, D and Pietinen, P (2000). Intake of flavonoids, carotenoids, vitamin C and E, and risk of stroke in male smokers. *Stroke* **31**: 2301-2306.
61. Rimm, EB, Katan, MB, Ascherio, A, Stampfer, MJ and Willett, WC (1996). Relation between intake of flavonoids and risk for coronary heart disease in male health professionals. *Ann. Intern. Med.* **125**: 384–389.
62. Yochum, L, Khushi, LH, Meyer, K and Folsom, AR (1999). Dietary flavonoid intake and risk of cardiovascular disease in postmanupausal women. *Am. J. Epidemiol.* **149**: 943–949.
63. Nakachi, K, Matsuyama, S, Miyaki, S, Suganuma, M and Imai, K (2000). Preventive effects of drinking green tea on cancer and cardiovascular disease: epidemiological evidence for multiple targeting prevention. *Biofactors* **13**: 49–54.
64. Sato, Y, Nakatsuka, H, Watanabe, T et al (1989). Possible contribution of green tea driking habits to the prevention of stroke. *Tohuku J. Exp. Med.* **157**: 337-343.
65. Keli, SO, Hertog, MG, Feskens, EJ and Kromhout, D (1996). Dietary flavonoids, antioxidant vitamins, and incidence of stroke: the Zutphen study. *Arch. Intern. Med.* **156**: 637–642.
66. Hivonen, T, Pietinen, P, Virtanen, M, Ovaskainen, M–L, Hakkinen, S, Albanes, D and Virtamo, J (2001). Intake of

flavonols and flavones and risk of coronary heart disease in male smokers. *Epidemiology* **12**: 62–67.

67. Knekt, P, Jarvinen, R, Reunanen, A and Maatela, J (1996). Flavonoid intake and coronary mortality in Finland: a cohort study. *Br. Med. J.* **312**: 478–481.
68. Hertog, MG, Feskens, EJ and Kromhout, D (1997). Antioxidant flavonols and coronary heart disease risk. *Lancet* **349**: 699.

Chapter 6

Anticarcinogenic Potential

Introduction

Annually, more than 5 million people are diagnosed with cancer and more than 3.5 million people die from cancer worldwide[1]. The inhibitory action of black and green teas their components against cancer initiation has been demonstrated in different animal models involving different organ sites in many laboratories[2, 3, 4]. Black tea has been shown to inhibit tumorogenesis in lung[5], colon[6] and skin[7] even though has not been convincingly detected in the blood. It has been reported[8] that oral administration of green and black tea or EGCG inhibited the growth of established nonmalignant and malignant skin tumours in tumour-bearing mice. Oral administration of black tea was also found to inhibit DNA synthesis and enhanced apoptosis in both nonmalignant and malignant tumours in tumour-bearing mice[9]. Evidences for the anticarcinogenic potential of tea polyphenols has been provided by numerous *in vitro* and experimental studies describing their action to bind directly to carcinogen inducing phase II enzymes such as UDP–glucuronosyl transferase and inhibiting heterocyclic amine formation. Molecular mechanisms, including catechin-mediated induction of apoptosis and cell cycle arrest, inhibition of transcription factors NF–kB and AP–1 and reduction of protein tyrosine kinase activity and *c-jun* mRNAexpression have also been suggested as relevant chemopreventive pathways adopted for tea[10].

Stomach Cancer

Among the various forms of cancer, stomach cancer is the second leading cause of mortality in the world[11]. Case control studies in Japan[12, 13] and China [14, 15] have suggested that consumption of eight or more cups of green tea per day at moderate temperature is beneficial. In Taiwan, a nonsignificant increase in the risk of gastric cancer among subjects who drank green tea habitually, as compared with those who did not[16]. In Japan, Shibata and coworkers reported[17] that consumption of more than 10 cups of green tea per day among 636 adults in a farming village reduced the risk of (OR = 0.63, 95 per cent CI: 0.43–0.93) precancerous chronic atrophic gastritis, even after adjustment for *Helicobacter pylori* and lifestyle factors associated with the condition. In addition, a nested case control study of gastric cancer in men of the Shanghai cohort in China with >4–year follow-up found an inverse correlation between urinary tea polyphenols and the risk of gastric cancer (OR = 0.52; 95 per cent CI = 0.28–0.97)[18]. Conversely, a population–based prospective cohort study of 26,311 Japanese adults found no association between green tea consumption and stomach cancer over an 8 years period[19]. However, the category consuming the largest quantity of green tea (5 or more cups) among this cohort was still lower in consumption levels than that utilised for other Asian cohorts, therefore the potential effect of greater intake, e.g., more than 7 to 10 cups a day, could not be distinguished. Sex, age, alcohol consumption, smoking, and other factors were considered during analysis of the data. No inverse association was also found by Hoshiyama and colleagues in Japan[20]. Again in Japan, Hoshiyama and coworkers[21] recently found no inverse association between the consumption of green tea and the risk of stomach cancer in a nested case-control study. After adjustment of age, smoking status, *Helicobacter pylori* infection, history of peptic ulcer, and family history of stomach cancer along with certain dietary elements, the risk associated with drinking one or two, three or four, five to nine, and ten or more cups of green tea per day relative to those drinking less than one cup per day were 1.3 (95 per cent CI: 0.6–2.8), 1.0 (95 per cent CI: 0.5–1.9), 0.8 (95 per cent CI: 0.4–1.6), and 1.2 (95 per cent CI: 0.6–2.5) respectively (p for trend = 0.899). Further, twenty-one epidemiological studies of green tea consumption in relation to gastrointestinal cancer, or preneoplastic lesions were identified recently through computerized literature searches and a protective effect of green tea on adenomatous polyps and chronic atrophic gastritis formations was suggested. But there was no clear epidemiological evidence to support the suggestion that green tea plays a role in the prevention of stomach and intestinal cancer[22].

Oesophageal Cancer

Any food consumed very hot can damage the oesophagus, and eventually lead to cancer of the oesophagus[23]. The consumption of tea has been considered a risk factor for oesophageal cancer (OC). Six publications reported a positive association between tea consumption and OC which has been attributed to the hot temperature of tea[24]. On the other hand, a population-based study conducted in Yangzhong, China, revealed that green tea consumers had 48 per cent and 51 per cent reduced risk of gastric cancer and chronic gastritis respectively[25]. In another population-based case-control study conducted in Shanghai, China, involving 734 OC patients, it was observed that the frequent consumption of green tea was associated with lower risk of OC particularly among nonsmokers and non-alcoholic drinkers[26]. In this study, five fold increase in the risk of OC was seen to be associated with drinking of very hot fluids, tea, soups and other drinks. Recently, in a Chinese study from a large hospital-based case-control for 1248 cases with oesophageal cancer and the same number of controls in South China showed that *Congou*, a grade of Chinese black tea, may protect against cancers of the oesophagus regardless of temperature when drinking[27]. Recently, the effects of several common dietary factors on the risk of squamous cell carcinoma of the oesophagus were examined in 284 male patients and 480 male controls of Taiwanese population.The results suggest that a high intake of preserved foods and overheated drinks might increase the risk of OC, and intake of fruits, vegetables, and tea might be negatively associated with the risk of OC[28].

In a prospective study of men conducted in China, direct evidences have suggested that tea polyphenols may act as a chemopreventive (chemoprevention is a strategy of disease control employing the use of diet and beverage containing naturally occurring or synthetic chemicals, vitamins, minerals that retard, block or reverse the disease process) agent against the development of gastric and oesophageal cancer[18].

Colorectal Cancer

Cooking meat and fish under normal conditions produces heterocyclic amine mutagens, several of which have been shown to induce colon tumours in experimental animals. Green as well as black tea inhibits the formation of pre-cancerous lesions, 'aberrant crypt foci' (ACF) induced in the large intestine of the rat by mutagens from cooked meat[29]. Using ACF as a biomarker, rats were treated with a mutagen from cooked meat (2–amino–3–methylimidazo [4, 5–f] quinoline, or 'IQ'), or with IQ plus green or black tea. 71 per cent of the animals given only the carcinogen developed ACF, whereas only 20 per cent of the rats given green tea and 33 per cent of the rats given black tea had ACF following treatment with carcinogen. Among those animals bearing ACF, an average of 2.4 ACF per colon were found in the group given only the carcinogen, compared with 1.0 ACF and 1.6 ACF per colon in rats given the carcinogen plus green tea or black tea respectively. Thus, both teas reduced the incidence and frequency of pre-cancerous lesions in the colon.

Preparation of tea has influence on the inhibitory activity[30]. It has been reported that most of the antimutagens were released from the tea leaves within 1–2 minutes of brewing. Fractionation of tea by HPLC showed that various catechins, including EGCG, EGC, and ECG were present in the tea extracts brewed for 1–2 minutes and accounted for most of the antimutagenic activity. Other components of tea, such as caffeine and tannins, were released in large quantities after prolonged brewing (3, 5, or 10 minutes), but these provided no inhibitory activity.[29] The preventive effect of green tea in pancreas, colon and rectal cancer was also reported[31]. Su and Arab have observed that tea consumption by men and women in the US significantly reduced the risk of colon cancer[32]. The Netherlands cohort study on diet and cancer found no association between black tea consumption and the risk of colorectal, stomach, lung or breast cancer in men or women[33]. In a population based case-control study (663 cases and 323 controls) on Moscow residents, an inverse association between tea intake and rectal cancer was found among Moscow women. The strength of the association reflects the method of exposure measurement. The difference between men and women in rectal cancer risk associated with tea intake may be partially explained by high alcohol consumption among Moscow men[34]. In a review, Arab and Il'yasova examined[35] the consistency of the effect of tea on colon cancer, rectal cancer or the formation of the premalignant lesion of colonic polyp formation in epidemiologic studies. They considered 30 papers and examined populations of 12 countries. In general, these studies did not provide consistent evidence to support that tea is a potent chemopreventive agent. A negative association was found stronger in observational epidemiologic studies of rectal cancer than in colon cancer. There was no consistent adjustment for important potential confounders of any tea relationship, such as consumption of coffee and alcohol and levels of physical activity. Further, in most of these studies the assessment of tea was based on a single question, and therefore, there was a possibility of having significant measurement error in comparison with the recent studies aimed at assessing consumption of tea.

Prostate Cancer

Prostate cancer (PC) is the most invasive, commonly diagnosed malignancy and the second largest cause of cancer-related deaths among men in the USA[36, 37]. In the Japanese and Chinese populations, which traditionally consume a low fat diet with several cups of tea, have one of the lowest rates of PC in the world. Similarly, the incidence of PC in India, a population that consumes tea regularly, is lower than in the western countries. The development and growth of PC is intimately associated with circulating androgen levels and the intracellular conversion of testosterone to the metabolically active 5 ∝-dihydrotestosteron[38]. The polyphenolic constituents of tea may act through alterations in either the androgen receptor or the converting enzyme 5 ∝-reductase. One published series found EGCG and ECG to be potent inhibitors of this converting enzyme[39], while another study demonstrated significant reduction in androgen-receptor mRNA levels and androgen-receptor promoter activity within LNCaP cells[40]. Administered *in vitro* to LNCaP cells (commercially available PC cell line), EGCG treatment has resulted in a dose-dependent decrease in PSA (prostate-specific antigen) levels within the supporting media[36]. *In vivo* apoptosis and growth inhibition of human PC cell lines LNCaP, PC–3 and DU145exposed to EGCG has also been demonstrated[41]. In animal studies that employ a transgenic adenocarcinoma of the mouse prostate (TRAMP), which is a model that mimics progressive forms of human prostate disease, it was observed that oral infusion of a polyphenolic fraction isolated from green tea (GTP) at a human achievable dose (equivalent to 6 cups of green tea/day) significantly inhibits PC development and metastasis[42].

It was also demonstrated that increased expression of genes related to angiogenesis such as vascular endothelial growth factor (VEGF) and those related to metastasis such as matrix metalloproteinases (MMP–2) and MMP-9 in prostate cancer of TRAMP mice. Oral feeding of GTP as the sole source of drinking fluid to TRAMP mice results in significant inhibition of VEGF, MMP–2 and MMP–9. These suggest that there are multiple targets for PC chemoprevention by green tea and highlight the need for further studies to identify novel pathways that may be modulated by green tea or its polyphenolic constituents that could be further exploited for prevention and/or treatment of PC[42].

There have been no prospective randomised trials examining PC prevention in humans through the administration of green or black tea. Recently, Hennings and coworkers assigned 20 men, all scheduled for radical prostatectomy, to drink either black, green tea or regular soda containing no tea polyphenols, five cups a day for five days before surgery[43]. The aim was to see if polyphenols found in tea might slow prostate cancer cell growth. Their blood serum was then collected and added to prostate tissue samples from LNCaP cells. Analysis of the prostate tissue showed a large variation in tea polyphenol content between study participants. When the proliferation of PC cells was measured, there was a significant decrease in the rate of appearance of new cancer cells in men who had consumed either green or black tea. The same was not found in those who had taken soda. This study suggests that both black and green tea are promising natural dietary supplements useful for chemoprevention of PC. Epidemiological studies suggest that green tea may reduce the incidence of clinically significant prostate tumours. Jain and coworkers used case (n = 617)-control (n = 637) method to examine the association between beverage intake and the risk of PC[44]. They found a slight decrease in PC risk in men consuming more than 500 g of tea (not specified as green tea) per day (OR: 0.70, 95 per cent CI: 0.50–0.99). Further, a case-control study was conducted recently in Hangzhou, South-east China to investigate the etiological association between PC and green tea consumption[45]. It was reported that PC risk declined with increasing frequency, duration and quality of green tea consumption. The adjusted odds ratio, relative to non-tea drinkers, were 0.28 (95 per cent CI = 0.17–0.47) for tea drinking, 0.12 (95 per cent CI = 0.06–0.26) for drinking tea for over 40 years, 0.09 (95 per cent CI = 0.04–0.21) for those consuming more than 1.5 kg of tea leaves in a year, and 0.27 (95 per cent CI = 0.15–0.48) for those drinking more than 3 cups (1 litre) daily. The dose response relationships were also significant, suggesting that green tea is protective against PC.

Phase II trial to explore anti-cancer effects of green tea in patients with androgen-independent prostate carcinoma was conducted in 2003[46]. In this trial, patients were instructed to take 6 grams of green tea per day orally in 6 divided doses and were monitored monthly for response and toxicity. The result of this study showed that tumour response, defined as a decline by 50 per cent in the baseline prostate-specific antigen (PSA) value, occurred in a single patient, or 2 per cent of the cohort. This trial concluded that green tea carries limited antineoplastic activity, as defined by a decline in PSA levels, among patients with androgen-independent prostate carcinoma. However, the patients selected for this clinical trial were of androgen-independent metastatic prostate carcinoma. Data in this study demonstrated that drinking green tea could not inhibit the progression of this type of prostate carcinoma at this late clinical stage[46]. It is therefore important to assess whether green tea has an inhibitory or chemopreventive effect on other cancers at various clinical stages.

Breast Cancer

In United States, *in vitro* assays and animal models demonstrated that green tea extracts (GTE) as well as its individual catechin components were effective in inhibiting breast cancer and endothelial cell proliferation[47]. In mouse experiments, GTE suppressed xenograft size and decreased the tumour vessel density. It was also investigated whether GTE inhibit vascular endothelial growth factor (VEGF) induction in human breast cancer cells. Inhibition of VEGF transcription appeared to be one of the molecular mechanism(s) involved in the antiangiogenic effects of green tea, which may contribute to its potential use for breast cancer treatment and/or prevention[48]. A population-based, case-control study on breast cancer was conducted among Chinese, Japanese and Filipino women in Los Angeles County and 501 breast cancer patients and 594 control subjects were interviewed[49]. The information on menstrual and reproductive factors; dietary habits including intake of black and green tea; and other lifestyle factors were considered during the study. It was found that risk of breast cancer was not related to black tea consumption. In contrast, green tea drinkers showed a significant reduced risk of breast cancer, and this was maintained after adjusting age, specific Asian ethnicity, birthplace, age at menarche, parity, menopausal status, use of menopausal hormones, body size and intake of total calories and black tea. The significant inverse association between risk of breast cancer and green tea intake remained after further adjustment for other potential confounders, like smoking; intake of alcohol,

Qualities of Green Tea as an Ideal Chemopreventive Agent

Many consumer products, including beverages, foods, health care products, and cosmetics, are now supplemented with extracts of green tea (see Box 4.1) indicating its acceptability to the humans. In addition to imparting preventive and therapeutic effects, green tea has also been shown to modulate and increase the efficacy of cancer chemotherapeutic drugs.

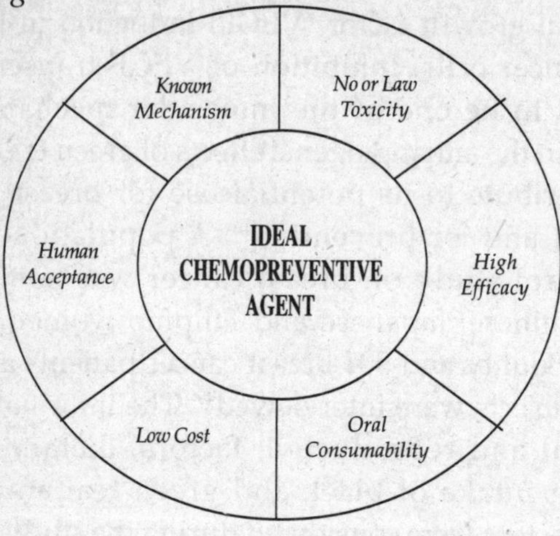

Box 6.1

Source: Ref. 10

coffee, black tea, soy and dark green vegetables; family history of breast cancer; and physical activity. Recently, in a pooled analysis of two prospective studies with 35004 Japanese women, green tea intake was not found associated with a lower risk of breast cancer (222 cases), the multivariate relative risk for women drinking $\geq$ 5 cups compared with <1 cup per day being 0.84 (95 per cent CI: 0.57-1.24, Trend $p = 0.69$)[50].

Bladder Cancer

Most of the earlier cohort studies did not observe a significant association between bladder cancer and tea consumption. Recently, an inverse association between black tea consumption and bladder cancer risk in men and women was observed after 6 years of follow up in a Netherlands Cohort Study[51]. A recent meta-analysis including 20 studies that evaluated tea consumption and urinary tract cancer risk, calculated a summary odds ratio of 1.01 (95 per cent CI: 0.92 to 1.01) of tea drinkers compared with nondrinkers[52]. In this meta-analysis, majority of studies evaluated only black tea consumption, the single cohort study and the two case-control studies that evaluated green tea consumption did not find significant associations between green tea consumption and bladder cancer risk. However, in a population-based case-control study of Americans, 30 per cent reduction in the risk of bladder cancer was associated with intake of more than five cups of tea per day[53]. But there was no evidence of a dose response relationship.

Skin Cancer

Effect of tea and tea polyphenols on the inhibition of skin tumorogenesis has been well studied. Early studies have demonstrated that topical application or ingestion of green and black tea polyphenols or EGCG inhibit tumour initiation and promotion of chemical carcinogens and UV light in mice[8, 54, 55]. Recent studies have indicated that caffeine may be an important constituent of tea in connection with the

How Many Cups of Tea Should One Drink?

Tea is a pleasant, popular, socially accepted, economical and safe drink that is enjoyed every day by hundreds of millions of people across all continents. 6 to 10 cups per day may be a useful dietary habit to assist in lowering the risk of a number of chronic diseases, especially as part of a health-promoting nutritional diet, low in total fat (emphasis on monosaturated and ω–3–polyunsaturated oils) and low in salt, with adequate vegetables and fruits, bran cereal insoluble fibre, and also sources of soluble fibre. Total fluid intake in adults might be about 2.5 litres, of which tea can contribute 0.7 to 1.4 litres. It has been observed that 650 ml of tea provides over half of the total requirement of dietary flanonoids; nearly 16 per cent of the daily requirement of calcium; almost 10 per cent of the daily requirement of zinc; over 10 per cent of the folic acid need; around 9 per cent, 25 per cent and 6 per cent of vitamins B1, B2 and B6 respectively (www.indiateaportal.com).

Box 6.2

Source: Ref. 70, 71

chemoprevention of UVB light-induced carcinogenesis[55, 56]. In some studies decaffeinated black tea enhanced the tumorigenesis induced by UVB light or a chemical promoter[54, 56], while in other studies reduction of tumorigenesis to a lesser extent than by whole tea extract has also been reported[54, 55].Topical application of polyphenolic fraction of green tea on mice skin papillomas can significantly decrease the conversion of benign tumours to malignant tumours[57]. Inhibition of growth of well established skin tumours by oral administration of green tea, black tea or EGCG has been reported and in some cases, tumour regression can be observed. Complete regression was reported in 4 per cent papilloma-bearing mice (n = 346)[8]. Significant decrease of growth of malignant tumours, squamous cell carcinomas and volume of tumours was observed when tumour bearing mice were fed with black tea. Enhancement in apoptosis and inhibition of DNA synthesis have been observed[8, 54]. In a population-based case-control study in Arizona, inverse association between tea consumption and the occurrence of squamous cell carcinoma of the skin was reported (OR = 0.33; 95 per cent CI: 0.12–0.87)[58].

Lung Cancer

Because cigarette smoking and tea drinking are very common behaviours in many diverse populations, several studies have explored the possible inhibitory effects of tea on lung cancer formation induced by cigarette smoking[59, 60]. Effect of green tea on biomarkers of oxidative stress in smokers and nonsmokers was investigated in volunteer study groups from China and United States. Green tea consumption in both groups decreased oxidative DNA damage (hydroxydeoxyguanosine (–OHdG) in white blood cells and urine), lipid peroxidation (MDA in urine), and free radical generation (2, 3–DHBA in urine) in smokers. Nonsmokers (US study group) also exhibited a decrease in overall oxidative stress[61]. Also, Misra and colleagues[62] studied the effect of black tea (BT) infusion on cigarette smoke (CS)–induced oxidative damage of proteins both *in vivo* and *in vitro*. In the *in vitro* experiment, BT prevented (P< 0.05) CS–induced oxidation of bovine serum albumin (BSA) and oxidative degradation of guinea pig lungs, liver and heart microsomal proteins. In the *in vivo* experiment, partially ascorbate-deficient guinea pigs were subjected to CS esposure from 5 cigarettes per guineapig/day for 7 days and given water or the BT infusion (20 g/L) to drink. In the guinea pigs who were exposed to CS and were given the BT infusion, higher reduction of the oxidation of microsomal proteins in lungs, liver and heart was observed in comparison with guinea pigs exposed to CS and given water. They also suggested that the results, if extrapolated to humans, would indicate that regular intake of tea may protect smokers from cigarette smoke-induced oxidative damage and the consequent degenerative diseases. Recently, a randomised controlled tea intervention trial was designed to study the effect of high consumption (4 cups per day) of decaffeinated green or black tea on oxidative DNA damage as measured by urinary 8–hydroxydeoxyguanosine (8–OHdG) among smokers over a 4 month–period. A total of 143 heavy smokers, aged 18–79 years old, were randomised to drink green tea, black tea, or water. Levels of plasma and urinary catechins and urinary 8–OHdG were measured monthly. A total of 133 of 143 smokers completed the

4-month intervention. Assessment of urinary 8–OHdG after adjustment for baseline measurements and other potential confounders revealed a highly significant decrease in urinary 8–OHdG (31 per cent) after 4 months of drinking decaffeinated green tea ($P = 0.002$). These data suggest that regular green tea drinking might protect smokers from oxidative damage and could reduce cancer risk or other diseases caused by free radicals associated with smoking[63].

Ovarian Cancer

It has been observed in a prospective cohort study conducted in the community, Hangzhou, China that increasing frequency and quantity of tea consumption was associated with a long survival of Chinese women with epithelial ovarian cancer[64]. Compared with non-drinkers, the adjusted hazard rlatios were 0.6 (95 per cent CI: 0.4–0.9) for tea drinkers, 0.3 (95 per cent CI: 0.2–0.8) for those consuming at least one cup of green tea per day, 0.4 (95 per cent CI: 0.2–0.8) for those brewing at least one batch of green tea per day, and 0.3 (95 per cent CI: 0.2–0.8) for those consuming 500 grams or more dried tea leaf per year. The corresponding dose response relationships were found statistically significant. This study has the potential to benefit women who are diagnosed with ovarian cancer.

There are multiple mechanisms by which tea constituents elicit their inhibitory effects against carcinogenesis These include, the modulation of signal transduction pathways that leads to the inhibition of cell proliferation and transformation, induction of apoptosis of preneoplastic and neoplastic cells, as well as inhibition of tumour invasion and angiogenesis[2]. However, these mechanisms needs to be evaluated and verified in animal and human models in order to get a clear understanding. Some of the previously reviewed and recent results on the protective cohort studies on tea consumption and cancer risk are summarised in Table 6.1. There are ample evidences from studies in cell culture and animal models which support the role of tea in protection against cancer. However, epidemiological studies have generated inconsistent results, some associating tea with reduced risk of cancer, whereas others claiming that tea lack protective activity against certain human cancers.

Yang and colleagues[65] identified some possible reasons for this difference which are: (1) tea may have a weak protective effect, which probably is masked by confounding factors associated with lifestyle in certain populations; (2) the amount of tea consumed by humans is much lower than the tea concentrations used in animal studies and therefore cannot produce a significant effect; and (3) tea inhibits carcinogenesis in animals by mechanisms that may not be applicable to the prevention of human cancer. To address these points, information on the active components, their bioavailability and tissue levels, and their mechanisms of actions is very important. However, a better perspective has been provided by Chung and coworkers on this controversy by summarising the laboratory studies on animals and humans with emphasis on animal tumour bioassays on skin, lung, mammary glands and colon, and the molecular and cellular mechanisms affected by tea[66].

Lambert and Yang recently proposed the possible cancer chemopreventive mechanisms of tea components based on *in vitro* and animal experiments. But their relevance *in vivo* needs to be demonstrated[67]. Arab and Il'yasova reviewed 30 studies [35] and failed to provide consistent evidence to support that tea is a potent chemopreventive agent. No convincing and consistent relationship between cancer incidence and tea consumption could be established by Ahmed and colleagues also[68]. It is seen that most of the case-control or cohort studies have not been specifically designed to examine the relationship between tea consumption and cancer incidence, and some studies reported in scientific literature do not adjust for cancer risk factors, e.g. smoking. Furthermore, in most of the studies, no adjustment has been made for confounding factors such as consumption of fruits and vegetables. It is noteworthy that in a population-based case-control study conducted in China, green tea consumption was found inversely correlated with pancreatic colorectal tumours after adjusting for smoking, fruit and vegetable consumption, etc. [30]. Moreover, attempt is also not made to adjust for the method of preparation of the tea (e.g. the strength of the infusion, temperature of the water, the addition of milk, lemon, etc.). Such factors may affect the nutritional quality of the tea brew. For example, the content of flavonoid of tea prepared using tea bags is higher than that prepared using loose leaves[69].

Further, work should continue on synthesizing and evaluating more analogs of tea polyphenols to find more potent, stable and specific polyphenol proteasome inhibitors as novel anti-cancer agents.[72, 73] This apart, scientists could direct their attention upon the diverse array of different natural and synthetic products as a complex mixture, a 'cocktail approach', which together may have synergistic anti-cancer benefits.[74] Different combinations of diverse agents could be tested including (–)-EGCG,[75] genistein[76, 77], selenium[78], curcumin[79], resveratrol[80], quercetin[81], extracts of apple and grape[82], and vitamin or mineral supplements[83]. This approach should continue to be explored in clinical, laboratory, animal, and epidemiological studies in the future. A major challenge of cancer prevention is to integrate new molecular findings into clinical practice[84]. Identification of molecular targets or biomarkers, whose changes are associated with inhibition of malignantly transformed cell properties, is paramount to cancer prevention and treatment by green/black tea and will greatly assist in a better understanding of anti-cancer mechanisms by tea drinking.

Table 6.1
Some prospective cohort studies on tea consumption and cancer risk

Country	*Subjects/ Events (Follow-up period)*	*Outcome: Association*	*RR (95 per cent CI)*	*Reference*
All cancers				
UK (Black tea)	14,085 men 1652 cancer deaths (19 y)	Positive	Observed deaths/expected 0–3 cups/d: 0.7; 4–6 cups/d: 0.8; 7–9 cups/d: 1.1 $\geq$ 10 cups/d: 1.2 P (trend) < 0.0001	85
US (Black tea)	128,934 men and women 1424 cancer deaths (10 y)	Non-significant	Tea as a continuous variable RR = 0.99 (per cup/day)	86
Netherlands (Flavonoids)	738 men 75 cancer cases (5 y)	Non-significant	$\geq$ 29.9 mg/d . $\leq$ 19 mg/d: RR= 1.21 (0.66–2.21)	88
US (Non-herbal tea)	35,369 postmenopausal women 2936 non-skin cancer cases (8 y)	Non-significant	Never/monthly: RR = 1.00 $\geq$ 2 cups/d: RR = 0.90 (0.76–1.07)	87
Japan (Green tea)	8522 men and women 384 cancer cases (9 y)	Inverse Significant for women only	Men $\geq$ 10 cups/d vs < 3 cups/d. RR = 0.68 (0.39–1.21) Women $\geq$ 10 cups/d vs < 3 cups/d: RR = 0.57 (0.33–0.98)	89

Country	*Subjects/ Events (Follow-up period)*	*Outcome: Association*	*RR (95 per cent Cl)*	*Reference*
Gastric Cancer				
US Hawaii (Black tea)	7833 men 136 deaths (20 y)	Non-significant	Age adjusted proportion of frequent black tea consumption (almost daily vs>daily): Stomach cancer deaths: 14.6 % Controls: 15.3%; P = 0.82	90
UK (Black tea)	14,085 men 172 deaths (19 y)	Positive	Observed deaths/expected 0–3 cups/d: 0.58; 4–6 cups/d: 0.76; 7–9 cups/d: 1.20; ≥ 10 cups/d: 1.44 P (trend) < 0.0005	91
Netherlands (Black tea)	58,279 men and 62,573 women 160 cases in men 40 cases in women (4.3 y)	Non-significant	≥ 5 cups/d vs 0 cups/d: RR = 0.94 (0.51–1.75)	33
US/Hawaii (Green tea and Black tea)	5233 men 6297 women 64 cases in men 44 cases in women (14.8 y)	Green tea: Non-significant	Green tea ≥ 2 cups/d vs 0 cup/d: RR = 1/5 (0.9–2.3)	92
		Non-significant	Black-tea: ≥ 1 cup/d vs 0 cup/d: RR = 0.8 (0.5–1.4)	
Japan (Green tea)	11,902 men 14,409 women 296 cases in men 123 cases in women (8 y)	Non-significant	≥ 5 cups/d vs < 1 cup/d: RR = 1.2 (0.9 –1.6)	19
Colorectal Cancer				
Netherlands (Black tea)	58,279 men 62,573 women 650 colorectal cancer cases (4.3 y)	Colorectal cancer: Non-significant	≥ 5 cups/d vs 0 cup/d: RR = 0.94 (0.66–1.34)	33
US (Non-herbal tea)	35,369 postmenopausal women 350 colon cancer cases 124 rectal cancer cases (8 y)	Colon cancer: Non-significant Rectal cancer: Non-significant	Colon cancer ≥ 2 cups/vs never/monthly RR = 0.71 (0.45–1.11) Rectal cancer ≥ 2 cups/d vs never/monthly: RR = 0.70 (0.34–1.46)	88
Finland (Black tea)	29,133 male smokers 111 colon cancer	Colon cancer: Positive	Colon cancer < 1 cup/d vs 0 cup/d: RR = 1.40 (0.84–2.33)	93

Country	Subjects/ Events (Follow-up period)	Outcome: Association	RR (95% CI)	Reference
	cases, 83 rectal cancer cases (8 y)	Rectal cancer: Non-significant	≥1 cup/d vs 0 cup/d: RR = 2.09 (1.34–3.26) Rectal cancer 1 cup/d vs 0 cup/d: RR = 0.87 (0.47–1.60)	
Pancreatic Cancer				
US (Black tea)	13,979 men and women 65 cases (9 y)	Inverse	1 cup/d vs < 1 cup/d: RR = 0.65 (0.31–1.37) ≥2 cups/d vs < 1 cup/d: RR = 0.37 (0.12–1.19) P (trend) < 0.05	94
US (Non-herbal tea) women 66 cases (9 y)	33,976 postmenopausal 66 cases (9 y)	Non-significant	> 1 cup/wk vs 0 cup/wk: RR = 0.92 (0.52–1.63)	95
US (Black Tea)	47,794 men 130 cases (12 y) 88,799 women 158 cases (16 y)	Non-significant for men, women, and pooled sample	Men 1 cup/d vs none: RR = 1.17 (0.61–2.22) Women 1 cup/d vs none: RR = 0.98 (0.60–1.60) Pooled 1 cup/d vs none: RR = 1.04 (0.71–1.54)	96
Lung cancer				
Netherlands (Black tea)	58,279 men and 62,573 women 764 cases (4.3 y)	Non-significant	≥5 cups/d vs 0 cup/d RR = 1.07 (0.73–1.57)	33
US (Non-herbal Tea)	35,369 postmenopausal women 312 cases (8 y)	Non-significant	≥2 cups/d vs never/monthly: RR = 1.05 (0.71–1.55)	88
Finland (Flavonoids)	9959 men and women 151 cases (143 men, 8 women) (20 y)	Inverse Tea was not a significant source of flanonoids)	Quartiles of flavonoid intake 1: (lowest): RR = 1.0 2: RR = 0.76 (0.50–1.16) 3: RR = 0.50 (0.29–0.85) 4: (highest): RR = 0.53 (0.29–0.97)	97
Netherlands (Catechins)	728 elderly men 42 lung cancer cases (10 y)	Non-significant for catechins	Tertile of total catechin intake Low: RR = 1.0 Medium: RR = 0.72 (0.33–1.56)	98

Country	*Subjects/ Events (Follow-up period)*	*Outcome: Association*	*RR (95% Cl)*	*Reference*
		and catechins from tea	High: RR = 0.92 (0.41–2.07)	
Bladder Cancer				
U.S. (Non-herbal tea)	35,369 postmenopausal women 43 cases (8 y)	Non-significant	$\geq$2 cups/d vs never/monthly: RR = 0.33 (0.08–1.35)	88
US (Black tea)	47,909 men 252 cases (10 y)	Non-significant	$\geq$2 cups/d vs < 1 cup/mo: RR = 0.69 (0.40–1.19) p (trend) = 0.08	99 100
Japan (Green tea and black tea)	38,450 atomic bomb survivors 114 cases (12–14 y)	Green tea: Non-significant Black tea: Non-significant	Green tea 5+ cups/d vs 0–1 cup/d: RR = 1.07 (0.58–2.08) Black tea 2+ cups/wk vs 0 cup/wk: RR = 0.81 (0.43–1.44)	
Netherlands (Black tea)	3123 men and women 569 cases (6 y)	Inverse	No tea vs 2-<3 cups/d: RR = 1.30 (0.96–1.78) <2 cups/d vs 2-<3 cups/d: RR = 0.95 (0.67–1.34) 3-<4 cups/d vs 2-<3 cups/d: RR = 0.81 (0.58–1.1.3) 4-<5 cups/d vs 2-<3 cups/d: RR = 0.81 (0.59–1.12) $\geq$5 cups/d vs 2-<3 cups/d: RR = 0.93 (0.66–1.30) P (trend) <0.01	51
Prostate Cancer				
Canada (Black tea)	3400 men 145 cases (20 y)	Non-significant	>750 ml/d vs 0 ml/d: RR = 1.13 (0.72–1.76)	101
Breast Cancer				
Netherland (Black tea)	62.573 women 507 cases (4.3 y)	Non-significant	4 cups/d vs non-drinker: RR = 1.31 (0.86–1.99)	33
US (Black tea)	35,369 postmenopausal women 1015 cases (8 y)	Non-significant	$\geq$2 cups/d vs never/monthly: R = 1.14 (0.92–1.41) P (trend) = 0.28	88

References

1. Ferlay, J, Bray, F, Pisani, P and Parkin, DM (2001). GLOBOCAN 2000: Cancer incidence, mortality and prevalence worldwide. In: *IARC Cancer base*. Version 1.0, IARC Press, Lyon, France.
2. Yang, CS, Maliakal, P and Meng, X (2002). Inhibition of carcinogenesis by tea. *Annu. Rev. Pharmacol. Toxicol.* **42**: 25–54.
3. Das, M, Sur, P, Gomes, A., Vedasiromoni, JR and Ganguly, D (2002). Inhibition of tumour growth and inflammation by consumption of tea. *Phytot. Res.* **16**: 40–44
4. Bhattacharya, A., Choudhuri, T, Pal, S., Chattopadhyay, S, Datta, GK, Sa, G and Das, T (2003). Apoptogenic effects of black tea on Ehrlich's ascites carcinoma cells. *Carcinogenesis* **24**: 75–80.
5. Hakim, I., Weisgerber, U., Harris, R, Balentine, D., van-Mierlo, C. and Paetau-Robinson, I. (2000). Preparation, composition and consumption patterns of tea-based beverages in Arizona. *Nutr. Res.* **20:** 1715-1724
6. Weisburger, JH, Rivenson, A., Reinhardt, J, Aliaga, C, Braley, J, Pittman, B and Zang, E (1998). *Carcinogenesis* **19:** 229–232
7. Javed, S, Mehrotra, NK and Shukla, Y (1998). Chemopreventive effects of black tea polyphenols in mouse skin model of carcinogenesis. *Biomed. Environ. Sci.* **11:** 307–313.
8. Conney, A.H, Lu, Y-P, Lou, Y–R, Xie, J–G. and Huang, MT 1999. Inhibitory effect of green and black tea on tumor growth. *Proc. Soc. Expl. Biol. Medicine* **220:** *229-233.*
9. Katiyar, SK (2001). Inhibition of photocarcinogenesis biomarkers by green tea polyphenols, (-)-epigallocatechin-3-gallate in human skin. *Proc. Intl. Conf. O-Cha (tea) Culture and Science*, Session III, Oct. 5–8, (2001), Shizuoka, Japan, 114–117.
10. Ahmad, N. and Mukhtar, H (1999). Green tea polyphenols and cancer: biologic mechanisms and practical implications. *Nutr. Rev.* **57**: 78–83.
11. Pisani, P, Parkin, DM and Ferlay, J (1993). Estimates of the worldwide mortality from eighteen major cancers in 1985:

implication for prevention and projections of future burden. *Intl. J. Cancer.* **55**: 891–903.

12. Kono, S, Ikeda, M, Tokudome, S and Kuratsune, M (1988). A case-control study of gastric cancer and diet in northern Kyushu, Japan. *Japan J. Cancer. Res* **79**: 1067–1074.
13. Inoue, M, Tajima, K and Hirose, K (1998). Tea and coffee consumption and the risk of digestive tract cancers: data from a comparative case-referent study in Japan. *Cancer Causes Control* **9**: 209–216.
14. Yu, GP, Hsieh, CC, Wang, LY, Yu, SZ, Li, XL and Jin, TH. Green-tea consumption and risk of stomach cancer: a population-based case control study in Shanghai, China. *Cancer Causes Control* **6**: 532–538.
15. Ji, BT, Chow, WH, Yang, G, McLaughlin, JK, Gao, RN, Zheng, W, Shu, XO, Jin, F and Fraumeni, JF Jr (1996). The influence of cigarette smoking, alcohol, and green tea consumption on the risk of carcinoma of the cardia and distal stomach in Shanghai, China. *Cancer* **77**: 2449–2457.
16. Lee, HH, Wu, HY and Chuang, YC (1990). Epidemiologic characteristics and multiple risk factors of stomach cancer in Taiwan. *Anticancer Res.* **10**: 875–881.
17. Shibata, K, Moriyama, M, Fukushima, T, Kaetsu, A, Miyazaki, M and Une, H (2000). Green tea consumption and chronic atrophic gastritis: a cross-sectional study in a green tea production village. *J. Epidemiol.* **10**: 310-316.
18. Sun, CL, Yuan, JM, Lee, M–J, Yang, CS, Gao, Y-T, Ross, RK and Yu, MC (2002). Urinary tea polyphenols in relation to gastric and esophageal cancers: a prospective study of men in Shanghai, China. *Carcinogenesis* **23**: 1497–1503.
19. Tsubono, Y, Nishino, Y, Komatsu, S., Hsieh, C., Kanemura, S, Tsuji, I, Nakatsuka, H, Fukao, A, Satoh, H and Hisamichi, S (2001). Green tea and risk of gastric cancer in Japan *N. Engl. J. Med.* **344**: 632–636.
20. Hoshiyama, Y, Kawaguchi, T, Miura, Y, Mizoue, T, Tokui, N, Yatsuya, H, Sakata, K, Kondo, T, Kikuchi, S, Toyoshima, H, Hayakawa, N, Tamakoshi, A, Ohno, Y and Yoshimura, T (2002). A prospective study of stomach cancer death in relation to green tea consumption in Japan. *British J. Cancer* **87**: 309–313

21. Hoshiyama, Y, Kawaguchi, T, Miura, Y, Mizoue, T, Tokui, N, Yatsuya, H, Sakata, K, Kondo, T, Kikuchi, S, Toyoshima, H., Hayakawa, N, Tamakoshi, A, Ohno, Y and Yoshimura, T (2004). A nested case-control study of stomach cancer in relation to green tea consumption in Japan. *British J. Cancer* **90**: 135–138.
22. Borrelli, F., Capasso, R, Russo, A. and Ernst, E (2004). Green tea and gastrointestinal cancer risk. *Alimentary Pharmacol. Therapeutics* **19**: 497–510.
23. Weisburger, JH. (1999). Tea and health: the underlying mechanisms. *Proc. Soc. Experimental Biology and Medicines* **220**: 271–275.
24. Wang, Z–Y, Chen, L, Lee, M–J, and Yang, CS (1996). Tea and cancer prevention. In: *Hypernutritious Food.* (eds.), Robinson, SF and Nagy, S, *Am. Chem. Soc. Symp.*, New Orleans, USA. pp. 239–260.
25. Setiawan, VW, Zhang, ZF, Yu G. P., Lu, QY, Li, YL, Lu, ML, Wang, MR, Guo, CH, Yu, SZ, Kurtz, RC and Hsieh, CC (2001). Protective effect of green tea on the risks of chronic gastritis and stomach cancer. *Intl. J. Cancer* **92**: 600–604.
26. Gao, YT, McLaughlin, JK, Blot, WJ, Ji, BT, Dai, Q and Fraumeni, JJ (1994). Reduced risk of oesophageal cancerassociated with green tea consumption. *J. Natl. Cancer Inst.* **86**: 855–858.
27. Ke, L, Yu, P, Zhang, ZX, Huang, SS, Huang, G, and Ma, XH (2002). *Congou* tea drinking and oesophageal cancer in South China. *British J. Cancer* **86**: 346–347.
28. Huang, H–C, Huang, M–C, Lee, J–M, Wu, D–C, Hsu, H–K. and Wu, M–T (2004). Association between diet and oesophageal cancer in Taiwan. *J. Gastroenterol. Hepatol.* 19: 632–637.
29. Dashwood, RH, Xu, M, Hernaez, JF, Hasaniya, N Youn, K and Razzuk, A (1999). Cancer chemopreventive mechanisms of tea against heterocyclic amine mutagens from cooked meat. *Proc. Soc. Expl. Biol. Medicine* **220**: 239-243.
30. Hernaez, J Xu–M and Dashwood, RH (1998). Antimutagenic activity of tea towards 2–hydroxyamino–3-methylimidazo [4,5–*f*] quinoline: Effect of tea

concentration and brew time on electrophile scavenging. *Mutat. Res.* **402**: 299–306.

31. Ji, BT, Chow, WH, Hsing, AW, McLaughlin, JK, Dai, Q, Gao, YT, Blot, WJ and Fraumeni, JFJr (1997). Green tea consumption and the risk of pancreatic and colorectal cancers. *Intl. J. Cancer* **70**: 255–258.
32. Su, LJ and Arab, L (2002). Tea consumption and the reduced risk of colon cancer results from a national prospective cohort study. *Public Health Nutr.* **5**: 419–425.
33. Goldbohm, RA., Hertog, MG, Brants, HA, van Poppel, G, and van den Brandt, PA (1996). Consumption of black tea and cancer risk: a prospective cohort study. *J. Natl. Cancer Inst.* **88**: 93–100.
34. Il'yasova, D, Arab, L, Martinchik, A, Sdvizhkov, A, Urbanovich, L and Weisgerber, U (2003). Black tea consumption and risk of rectal cancer in Moscow population. *Ann. Epidemiol.* **13**: 405–411.
35. Arab, L and Il'yasova, D (2003). The epidemiology of tea consumption and colorectal cancer incidence. *J. Nutr.* **133**: 3310S–3318S.
36. Gupta, S, Ahmad, N and Mukhtar, H (1999). Prostrate cancer chemoprevention by green tea. *Semin. Urol. Oncol.* **17**: 70–76.
37. Anonymous, (2002). Cancer facts and figures. *American Cancer Society Inc.*, Atlanta, GA, USA.1-45.
38. Ward, JF and Blute, ML (2003). Chemoprevention of prostrate cancer. *Expert Rev. Anticancer Ther.* **3**: 203-214
39. Liao, S. and Hiipakka, RA (1995). Selective inhibition of steroid 5 alpha-reductase isozymes by tea epicatechin–3–gallate and epigallocatechin–3–gallate. *Biochem. Biophys. Res. Commun.* **214**: 833–838.
40. Ren, F, Zhang, S, Mitchell, SH, Butler, R and Young, CYF (2000). Tea polyphenols down-regulate the expression of the androgen receptor in LNCaP prostrate cancer cells. *Oncogene* **19**: 1924–1932.
41. Paschka, AG, Butler, R and Young, CY (1998). Induction of apoptosis in prostrate cancer cell lines by the green tea component, (–)–epigallocatechin–3–gallate. *Cancer Lett.* **130**: 1–7.

42. Adhami, VM, Ahmad, N and Mukhtar, H (2003). Molecular targets for green tea in prostrate cancer prevention. *J. Nutr.* **133**: 2417S–2424S.
43. Hennings, SM, Niu, Y, Lee, NH, Conde, F, Leung, P, Hong, J, Çsathy, G, Ziaee, HG, Go, VLW, Heber, D and Aronson, WJ (2004). Bioavailability and bioactivity of tea polyphenols in human prostate tissue and serum after green and black tea consumption. *Paper presented at the Experimenta Biology 2004 Meeting* held in Washingtong DC from April 17–21, 2004.
44. Jain, MG, Hislop, GT, Howe, GR, Burch, JD and Ghadirian, P (1998). Alcohol and other beverage use and prostrate cancer risk among Canadian men. *Int. J. Cancer* **78**: 707–711.
45. Jian, L, Xie, L–P, Lee, AH and Binns, CW (2004). Protective effect of green tea against prostate cancer: a case-control study in southeast China. *Intl. J. Cancer* **108:** 130–135.
46. Jatoi, A, Ellison, N, Burch, PA., Solan, JA, Dakhil, SR, Novotny, P, Tan, W, Fitch, TR, Rowland, KM, Young, CY and Flynn, PJ (2003). A phase II trial of green tea in the treatment of patients with androgen independent metastatic prostrate carcinoma. *Cancer* **97**: 1442–1446.
47. Sartippour, MR, Heber, D, Ma, Z, Lu, Q Go, VL and Nguyen, M (2001). Green tea and its catechins inhibit breast cancer xenografts. *Nutr. Cancer* **40**: 149–156.
48. Sartippour, MR, Shao, Z, Heber, D, Beatty, P, Zhang, L, Liu, C, Ellis, L, Liu, W, Go, VL and Brooks, MN (2002). Green tea inhibits vascular endothelial growth factor (VEGF) induction in human breast Cancer cells. *J. Nutr.* **132**: 2307–2311.
49. Wu, AH, Yu, MC, Tseng, C–C, Hankin, J and Pike, MC (2003). Green tea and risk of breast cancer in Asian Americans. *Intl. J. Cancer* **106**: 574–579.
50. Suzuki, Y, Tsubono, T, Nakaya, N., Suzuki, Y, Koizumi, Y and Tsuji, I (2004). Green tea and the risk of breast cancer: pooled analysis of two prospective studies in Japan. *Br. J. Cancer* **90**: 1361–1363.
51. Zeegers, MP, Dorant, E, Goldbohm, RA and van den Brandt, PA (2001). Are coffee, tea, and total fluid consumption associated with bladder cancer risk? Results

from the Netherlands Cohort Study. *Cancer Causes Control* **12**: 231–238.

52. Zeegers, MP, Tan, FE, Goldbohm, RA and van den Brandt, PA (2001). Are coffee and tea consumption associated with urinary tract cancer risk? A systematic review and meta-analysis. *Int. Rev. Epidemiol.* **30**: 353–362
53. Bianchi, G, Cerhan, J, Parker, A., Putnam, S., See, W., Lynch, C and Cantor, K (2000). Tea consumption and risk of bladder and kidney cancers in a population-based case–control study. *Am. J. Epidemiol.* **151**: 377–383.
54. Lu, Y–P, Lou, Y–R, Xie, P, Yen, M–T, Huang, AH and Conney, A.H (1997). Inhibitory effect of black tea on the growth of established skin tumors in mice: effects on tumor size, apoptosis, mitosis and bromodeoxyuridine incorporation into DNA. *Carcinogenesis* **18**: 2163-2169.
55. Wang, ZY, Huang, MT, Lou, YR, Xie, JG, Reulh, KR, Newmark, HL Yang, CS and Conney, AH (1994). Inhibitory effects of black tea, green tea, decaffeinated black tea, and decaffeinated green tea on ultraviolet B light-induced skin carcinogenesis in 7, 12–dimethylbenz[a] anthracene-intiated SKH-1 mice. *Cancer Res.* **54**: 3428–3435.
56. Huang, MT, Xie, JG, Wang, ZY, Ho, CT, Lou, YR, Wang, CX, Hard, GC and Conney, AH (1997). Effects of tea, decaffeinated tea, and caffeine on UVB light-induced complete carcinogenesis in SKH-1 mice: demonstration of caffeine as a biologically important constituent of tea. *Cancer Res.* **57**: 2623–2629.
57. Katiyar, SK, Agarwal, R and Mukhtar, H (1993). Protection against malignant conversion of chemically induced benign skin papillomas to squamous cell carcinomas in SENCAR mice by a polyphenolic fraction isolated from green tea. *Cancer Res.* **53**: 5409–5412.
58. Hakim, I, Harris, R and Weisgerber, U (2000). Tea intake and squamous cell carcinoma of the skin: Influence of type of beverages. *Cancer Epidemiol. Biomarkers Prev.* **9**: 727–731.
59. Xu, Y, Ho, CT, Amin, SG, Han, C and Chung, FL(1992). Inhibition of tobacco–specific nitrosamine-induced lung tumerogeneiss in A/J mice by green tea and its major polyphenol as antioxidants. *Cancer Res.* **52**: 3875–3879.

60. Yang, CS and Yang, ZY (1993). Tea and cancer. *J. Natl. Cancer Inst*. **85**: 1038–1049.
61. Klaunig, JE, Xu, Y, Han, C, Kamendulis, LM, Chen, J, Heiser, C, Gordon, MS and Mohler, ER (1999). The effect of tea consumption on oxidative stress in smokers and nonsmokers. *Proc. Soc. Expl. Biol. Medicine* **220**: 249–254.
62. Misra, A, Chattopadhyay, R, Banerjee, S, Chattopadhyay, DJ and Banerjee, IB (2003). Black tea prevents cigarette smoke induced oxidative damage of proteins in Guinea pig *J. Nutr.* **133**: 2622–2628.
63. Hakim, IA, Harris, RB, Brown, S, Sherry Chow, H-H, Wiseman, S, Agarwal, S and Talbot, W (2003). Effect of increased tea consumption on oxidative DNA damage among smokers: a randomized controlled study. *J. Nutr.* **133**: 3303S–3309S.
64. Binns, CW, Zhang, M, Lee, AH and Xie, CX (2004). Green tea consumption enhances survival of epithelial ovarian cancer patients. *Asia Pac. J. Clin. Nutr.* **13**(S): S116.
65. Yang, CS, Chung, J–Y, Yang, G, Chhabra, SK and Lee, M (2000). Tea and tea polyphenols in cancer prevention. *J. Nutr*. **130**: 472S-478S.
66. Chung, F-L, Schwartz, J, Herzog, CR and Yang, Y–M (2003). Tea and cancer prevention: studies in animals and humans. *J. Nutr.* **133**: 3268S-3274S.
67. Lambert, JD and Yang, CS (2003). Mechanisms of cancer prevention by tea constituents. *J. Nutr.* **133**: 3262S–3267S.
68. Ahmed, N, Katiyar, SK and Mukhtar, H (1998). Cancer chemoprevention by tea polyphenols. In: *Nutrition and Chemical Toxicity*. (ed.), Ioannides, C; John Wiley & Sons, Chichester, pp. 301-343.
69. Hertog, MGL, Feskens, EJM, Hollman, PCH, Katan, MB, and Kromhout, D (1993). Dietary antioxidant flavonoids and the risk of coronary heart disease: the Zutphen Elderly Study. *Lancet*, **342**: 1007–1011.
70. Weisburger, JH. 2002. Lifestyle, health, and disease prevention: the underlying mechanisms. *Eur. J. Cancer Prev.* **11**(Suppl. 2): S1–S7.
71. Weisburger, JW (2003). Tea and Health. In: *Herbal Medicine & Molecular Basis in Health and Disease Management*. (eds.)

Packer, L, Halliwell, B, Ong, CN; Mercel Dekker, Inc, New York. 117–144.

72. Smith, DM, Daniel, KG, Wang, Z, Guida, WC, Chan, TH and Dou, QP (2004). Docking studies and model development of tea polyphenol proteasome inhibitors: Applications to rational drug design. *Proteins: Structure, Function, and Genetics* **54**: 58–70.
73. Smith, DM, Wang, Z, Kazi, A, Li, LH, Chan, TH and Dou, QP (2002). Synthetic analogs of green tea polyphenols as proteasome inhibitors. *Mol. Med.* **8**: 382–392.
74. Nam, S, Smith, DM and Dou, QP (2001). Ester bond-containing tea polyphenols potently inhibit proteasome activity *in vitro* and *in vivo*. *J. Biol. Chem.* **276**: 13322-13330.
75. Mukhtar, H and Ahmad, N (1999). Cancer chemoprevention: future holds in multiple agents. *Toxicol. Appl. Pharmacol.* **158**: 207–210.
76. Kazi, A, Daniel, KG, Smith, DM, Kumar, NB and Dou QP (2003). Inhibition of the proteasome activity, a novel mechanism associated with the tumor cell apoptosis inducing ability of genistein. *Biochem. Pharmacol.* **66**: 965–976.
77. Kim, H, Peterson, TG and Barnes, S (1998). Mechanisms of action of the soy isoflavone genistein: emerging role for its effects via transforming growth factor beta signaling pathways. *Am. J. Clin. Nutr.* **68** (Suppl): 1418S–1425S.
78. Ganther, HE (1999). Selenium metabolism, selenoproteins and mechanisms of cancer prevention: complexities with thioredoxin reductase. *Carcinogenesis* **20**: 1657–1666.
79. Jiang, MC, Yang-yen, H–F, Yen, JJ and lin, JK (1996). Curcumin induces apoptosis in immortalized NIH 3T3 and malignant cancer cell lines. *Nutr. Cancer* **26**: 111-120.
80. Hsieh, TC and Wu, JM (1999). Differential effects on growth, cell cycle arrest, and induction of apoptosis by resveratrol in human prostate cancer cell lines. *Exp. Cell Res.* **249**: 109–115.
81. Morrow, DM, Fitzsimmons, PE, Chopra, M and McGlynn, H (2001). Dietary supplementation with the anti-tumour promoter quercetin: its effects on matrix metalloproteinase gene regulation. *Mutat. Res.* **480–481**: 269–276.

82. Chen, MS, Chen, D and Dou, QP. (2004). Inhibition of the proteasome activity by various fruits and vegetables is associated with cancer cell death. *In Vivo* 18: 73–80.
83. White, E, Patterson, RE, Kristal, AR, Thornquist, M, King, I., Shattuck, AL, Evans, I., Satia-Abouta, J, Littman, AJ and Potter, JD (2004). Vitamins and lifestyle cohort study: study design and characteristics of supplement users. *Am. J. Epidemiol.* **159**: 83–93.
84. Chen, D, Daniel, KG, Kuhn, DJ, Kazi, A., Bhuiyan, M, Li, L, Wang, Z, Wan, SB, Lam, WH, Chan, TH and Dou, QP (2004). Green tea and tea polyphenols in cancer prevention. *Frontiers Biosci.* **9**: 2618–2631.
85. Kinlen, LJ, Willows, AN, Goldblatt, P and Yudkin, J (1988). Tea consumption and cancer. *Br. J. Cancer* 58**:** 397–401.
86. Klatsky, AL, Armstrong, MA and Friedman, GD (1993). Coffee, tea and mortality. *Ann. Epidemiol.* **3**: 375–338.
87. Hertog, MG, Feskens, EJ, Hollman, PC, Katan, MB and Kromhout, D (1994). Dietary flavonoids and cancer risk in the Zutphen Elderly Study. *Nutr. Cancer* **22**: 175–184.
88. Zheng, W, Doyle, TJ, Kushi, LH, Sellers, TA., Hong, CP and Folsom, AR (1996). Tea consumption and cancer incidence in a prospective cohort study of post menuposal women. *Am. J. Epidemiol.* **144**: 175–182.
89. Imai, K, Suga, K and Nakachi, K (1997). Cancer-preventive effects of drinking green tea among a Japanese population. *Prev. Med.* **26**: 769–775.
90. Heilbrun, LK, Nomura, A. and Stemmermann, GN (1986). Black tea consumption and cancer risk a prospective study. *Br. J. Cancer* **54**: 677–683.
91. Kinlen, LJ, Willows, AN, Goldblatt, P and Yudkin, J (1988). Tea consumption and cancer. *Br. J. Cancer* **58**: 397-401.
92. Galanis, DJ, Kolonel, LN, Lee, J and Nomura, A (1998). Intakes of selected food and beverages and the incidence of gastric canceramong the Japanese residents of Hawaii: a prospective study. *Int. J. Epidemiol.* **27**: 173–180.
93. Hartman, TJ, Tangrea, JA., Pietinen, P, et al (1998). Tea and coffee consumption and risk of colon and rectal cancerin middle-aged Finnish men. *Nutr. Cancer* **31**: 41–48.
94. Shibata, A, Mack, TM, Paganini–Hill, A, Ross, RK and Henderson, BE (1994). A prospective study of pancreatic cancer in the elderly. *Int. J. Cancer* **58**: 46–49.

95. Harnack, LJ, Anderson, KE, Zheng, W, Folsom, AR, Sellers, TA and Kushi, LH (1997). Smoking, alcohol, coffee, and tea intake and incidence of cancer of the exocrine pancreas: the Iowa Women's Health Study. *Cancer Epidemiol. Biomarkers. Prev.* **6**: 1081–1086.
96. Michaud, DS, Giovannucci, E, Willett, WC, Colditz, GA and Fuchs, CS (2001). Coffee and alcohol consumption and the risk of pancreatic cancer in two prospective United States cohorts. *Cancer Epidemiol. Biomarkers Prev.* **10**: 429–437.
97. Knekt, P, Jarvinen, R, Seppanen, R, Hellovaara, M, Teppo, L, Pukkala, E and Aromma, A (1997). Dietary flavonoids and the risk of lung cancer and other malignant neoplasms. *Am. J. Epidemiol.* **146**: 223–230.
98. Arts, IC, Hollman, PC, Bueno D Mesquita, HB, Feskens EJ and Kromhout, D (2001). Dietary catechins and epithelial ncancer incidence: the Zutphen elderly study. *Int. J. Cancer* **92**: 298–302.
99. Michaud, DS, Spiegelman, D, Clinton, SK, Rimm, EB, Curhan, GC, Willett, WC and Giovannucci, EL (1999). Fluid intake and the risk of bladder cancer in men. *N. Engl. J. Med.* **340**: 1390–1397.
100. Nagano, J, Kono, S, Preston, DL, Moriwaki, H, Sharp, GB, Koyama, K and Mabuchi, K (2000). Bladder cancer incidence in relation to vegetable and fruit consumption: a prospective study atomic-bomb survivors. *Int. J. Cancer* **86**: 132–138.
101. Ellison, LF (2000). Tea and other beverage consumption and prostate cancer risk: a Canadian retrospective cohort study. *Eur. J. Cancer Prev.* **9**: 125–130.

Chapter 7

Protective Effects of Tea

Antibacterial Effects

Regular intake of tea and tea polyphenols has health promoting effects on the intestinal bacterial flora. It favours the outgrowth of beneficial bacteria (*Lactobacilli* and *Bifidobacteria*) in the intestinal tract and decreases the development of less beneficial bacteria (*Enterobacteriaceae*), thus changing the nature of the intestinal bioflora[1]. *Enterobacteriaceae* in the intestinal tract have mostly unpleasant properties since they generate smelly chemicals of the type of skatole and related indoles. A study on faecal conditions of elderly residents in a long-term care facility indicated that tea catechins can significantly improve bowel activity[2]. Remarkable improvements in bowel conditions were also reported in animals as well as in humans by the administration of tea catechins equivalent to only 5–6 cups per day of tea[3]. The modulation activity of tea on the intestinal microflora has been demonstrated[4]. Studies with animals indicated that tea theaflavins and thearubigins do have biological activities even though the bioavailability of these compounds is not known. It is possible that these black tea polyphenols are converted by intestinal microbes to compounds that are bioavailable and bioactive[5].

Tea extracts exhibit inhibitory effects against *Vibrio cholerae*, *Salmonella typhi*, *Campilobacter jejuni*, *Campilobacter coli*, *Helicobacter pylori*, *Shigella*, *Clostridium*, *Pseudomonas*, *Candida*, *Mycoplasma*, and *Cryptococcus*[6-9]. The latter is responsible for gastric and duodenal ulcers that can induce cancer[10].

In general, gram positive bacteria are more sensitive to tea extracts than gram negative bacteria[11] Tea can inhibit the growth of *Staphylococcus aureus* and *Vibrio parahaemolyticus* responsible for cholera and diarrhoeal diseases, and it can reverse the methicillin-resistance in *Staphylococci*[11–12]. Aqueous extracts of black tea along with their respective methanol extracts were found to possess *in vitro* amoebicidal action against trophozoites of *Entamoeba histolytica* under axenic conditions. Aqueous tea extracts were also found to inhibit the growth of *Escherichia coli* over nutrient agar. These results indicate that selective amoebicidal action can be achieved with tea extract which hinders proliferation of amoebae without destroying the normal bacterial flora of the intestine[13]. Aqueous tea extracts contain factors which can reverse the aflatoxin toxicity of *Bacillus megaterium*[14] and inhibit extracellular release of vero toxin from enterohemorrhagic *Escherichia coli*[15]. The antibacterial activity of oolong tea extract on oral streptococci, including *Streptococcus mutants* and *S sobrinus* was determined and highest activity was found against *S mutants* MT8148R[16]. It was suggested that the antibacterial activity is caused by a synergistic effect of monomeric polyphenols, which can easily bind to proteins.

Antiviral Effects

Tea polyphenols have antiviral actions, as described in detail in the monograph of Hara[3]. Multiplication of A & B type influenza virus is effectively inhibited by rinsing out the mouth with a concentration of black tea extract[17]. Catechins have an inhibitory effect on the multiplication of viruses including human immunodeficiency virus (HIV). In HIV–1 infection, EGCG is responsible for the reported antiviral effects of green tea[18–20]. Several mechanisms for the antiviral effects of EGCG on HIV–1 have been proposed. EGCG inhibits HIV–1 replication in human PBMCs *in vitro* by inhibiting the biochemical activity of HIV–1 reverse transcriptase, the result being a subsequent decrease in HIV p24 antigen concentration[19]. Another study shows that EGCG interferes with HIV–1 viral infection by virion destruction and HIV–1 reverse transcriptase inhibition[20]. Finally, EGCG induces virion destruction *in vitro* by deformation of phospholipids via binding to the surface of the viral envelope[21]. Kawai *et al* have reported[18] yet another anti-HIV–1 effect of EGCG, one that prevents the attachment of the HIV–1 virion, gp120, to CD4 molecules on T–helper cells. The researchers found that in human CD4 T cells, EGCG (25–250 µmol/L) downregulated the cell surface expression of CD4 by binding to the CD4 molecule, presumably at a binding site recognised by gp120. Alternate explanations for this theory were ruled out by the demonstrated absence of (1) CD4 shedding from the cell surface, b (2) loss of CD4 molecules, and (3) CD4 endocytosis[20, 22]. Further, additional studies to better define the nature and specificity of EGCG binding to the CD4 molecule have been suggested[20]. Recently, a model of EGCG binding to a pocket of the CD4 molecule with competitive inhibition of HIV–1–gp 120 binding has been proposed.[23] Effects of EGCG on HIV infection were also determined by incubating peripheral blood lymphocytes with either LAI/IIIB or Bal HIV strains and increasing concentrations of EGCG. EGCG was found to strongly inhibit the replication of both virus strains as determined by reverse transcriptase and p24 assays on the cell supernatants[20].

Adenoviruses are implicated in a variety of human and animal pathologies and are currently under intensive investigation as gene transfer vectors. While studying the effect of EGCG on the inhibition of adenovirus infection and the viral protease adenain in cell culture, Weber and colleagues found[24] that anti-adenoviral activity of EGCG manifests itself through several mechanisms, both outside and inside the cell, but at effective drug concentrations well above that reported in the serum of green tea drinkers. However, the antimicrobial activity of tea in humans is not well documented and should be studied in multi-dimensional way since various mechanisms, viz. the immune system, heredity, cell biology, microbial ecology, environment are involved. Recently, it was reported that intake of 4–5 cups of black tea for 4 weeks led to an increase of γ–δ lymphocytes and in turn of γ-interferon, reflecting a raised immune response[25].

Anticariogenic Action

Tea components have been shown to possess some anticaries activity[26]. Drinking of tea was found to be associated with lower levels of dental caries in a cross-sectional study of 6,014 secondary school children in UK, regardless of whether they added sugar to their tea or not[27]. Current researches have provided incontrovertible evidence that tea drinking not only reduces plaque build-up but also helps control growth of bacteria such as *Escherichia coli, Streptococcus salivarius* and *S mutans* on teeth[3, 16, 28-29]. Tea polyphenols are anticariogenic in three ways: (1) they inhibit the plaque forming enzyme, (2) they suppress the growth of *S mutans*, and (3) they solidify the enamel[3]. EGCG also inhibits the growth and adherence of *Porphyromonas gingivalis* bacteria responsible for periodontal disease[30, 31] .

Sugared and acidic soft drinks have been implicated in causing dental caries and erosion[32]. The question is whether the acidity of tea is likely to erode teeth. After drinking black tea the pH profile at the palatal surface of anterior and posterior sites of the dentition was determined[32] and it was reported that the pH of the tea solution was 4.9 and the major anions detected were oxalate and citrate. Tooth surface pH monitoring indicated a very small decrease of less than 1 pH unit after drinking tea and minimum mean pH reached was 5.45. After 20–25 seconds, maximum decrease in pH was observed. This indicated that tea may be safely recommended as a substitute for more acidic drinks as a part of preventive measures against dental erosion.

Bad breath or halitosis afflicts a large portion of the population. It is caused by foul-smelling volatile sulphur compounds, like hydrogen sulphide (H_2S), produced by anaerobic bacteria that thrive in environments lacking oxygen, such as the back of the tongue and deep gum pockets. In a laboratory study conducted by Zhu and coworkers, purified tea polyphenols were incubated for 48 hours with bacteria, viz. *Porphyromonas gingivalis* (Pg) and *Fusobacterium nucleatum* which are associated with bad breath[33]. At concentrations ranging from

16 to 250 micrograms/ml, the polyphenols inhibited the growth of oral bacteria. At even lower concentrations ranging from 2.5 to 25 micrograms/ml, the polyphenols hindered the enzymes that catalyse the formation of H_2S, lowering its production by 30 per cent. This study complements earlier research showing that black tea supressess growth of bacteria in dental plaque and that rinsing with black tea reduces plaque formation and the production of acids that cause tooth decay.

Tea extracts have been used as an additive to the toothpastes for the purpose of preventing dental caries. The antiviral and antibacterial effect of several oral agents (i.e., Colgate, Aquafresh, Aim, Crest and Orajel toothpastes) was found enhanced by the addition of green[34] and white tea[35] extracts. It was also reported that in the absence of these extracts, the oral agents had very little effect, whereas with the addition of the extract a 99 per cent loss of phage titer and in some cases, total inactivation of bateriophage T1 was obtained. These studies indicate that green and white tea extract may have a role in the inactivation of microbial pathogen. Now–a–days, green tea extracts are being sold in Japan for their ability to diminish mouth odour. Candy and chewing gum containing green tea extract are also sold in the confectionery market as dental care candy and tooth deodorants.

Fluoride is needed to protect the teeth against dental caries[36] and to support bone mineralisation. The tea plant extracts fluoride from the soil, which then accumulates in its leaves. Tea is a very rich source of fluoride. Dry tea leaves may contain 4-400 ppm fluoride, the brewed tea 0.34–6 ppm resulting in one cup of tea containing between 0.3 mg and 0.5 mg of fluoride (http://*www.teahealth.co.uk*). Simpson and coworkers investigated[37] the bio-availability of fluoride from black tea in relation to its interaction with the tooth surface and oral tissues, and demonstrated that after rinsing with tea, 34 per cent fluoride was retained in the oral cavity and that some of this showed a strong binding ability to enamel particles on the tooth surface. It was opined that the tea is an effective vehicle for delivering fluoride to the the oral cavity where it may then become associated with the oral tissues potentially helping to prevent dental decay.

Tannin is another component of tea that can inhibit amylase in human saliva thereby reducing the cariogenic potential of starch containing foods such as crackers and cakes[38]. A number of studies have also demonstrated that tannic acid inhibits the growth of *S mutans* bacteria[39-41], a major factor in the build-up of dental plaque. This apart, tannin, along with other components of tea such as catechins, caffeine and tocopherol, has been shown to be effective in increasing the acid resistance of tooth enamel[42].

Bone Health

Fractures (in particular, hip fractures) are one of the leading causes of ill health in older men and women. Although many risk factors have been documented for hip fractures[43, 44], osteoporosis, or low bone mineral density (BMD), is the single most important known risk factor for fracture in older women[43]. It was reported that the older British women who drank tea had higher BMD measurements at the lumbar spine and hip than non drinkers[45]. These findings were independent of other factors known to affect BMD (e.g., smoking and hormone replacement therapy), and whether milk was added to the tea. Further, two large case-control studies in Mediterranean countries found low tea consumption to be significantly and independently associated with an increased risk of hip fractures in men and women over 50 years of age[46, 47]. Positive associations between tea drinking and BMD of the lumbar or the femoral neck region were also reported[45, 48]. Hernandez and coworkers reported a weak inverse association between ultradistal BMD and tea intake in pre- and perimenopausal women in a subset of the Massachusetts Women's Health Study[49]. Tea drinking may protect against osteoporosis in older women. Recently, it was observed that habitual tea drinkers of 6 to 10 years had hip bone density 2.3 per cent higher than non-habitual tea drinkers[50]. Habitual tea drinkers had significant beneficial effects on BMD of the total body, lumbar spine, and hip regions in adults. Chen and colleagues investigated[51] association of habitual regular tea drinker with BMD and fracture risk. The participants were a multiethnic postmenopausal cohort (50 to 79 years of age) from the nationwide Women's Health Initiative Observational Study in the United States. This study did not show any significant association between tea drinking and the risk of fractures at the hip and forearm/wrist. They suggested for inclusion in future studies the detailed assessments of tea consumption to delineate whether various tea preparations and types of tea, such as green versus black, have different contribution to BMD measurements and the risk of fractures.

The mechanisms for the beneficial effect of tea consumption on BMD however are not clear. Although tea is a relatively good source of fluoride, an element known to increase bone density in pharmacologic doses, there is little evidence that the amount of fluoride supplied by tea would significantly affect BMD[52]. In a cross-sectional study of 101 men and women, the oxidative stress-responsive transcription factor, NF-kB has been found to play a role in bone resorption, and increased levels of urinary 8–iso–PGF_{2k}, a biomarker for oxidative stress, were significantly associated with decreased lumbar spine and total body BMD[53].

However, tea polyphenols could preserve BMD through estrogenic effects, by decreasing oxidative stress, or by altering gene expression. Further studies are required to determine whether tea consumption affects the development of osteoporosis or the risk of osteoporotic fracture in a meaningful way.

Kidney Stone

In a randomised double cross over study, ten volunteers consumed six cups of two brands of black teas (6.1 and 6.3 mg soluble oxalate/g tea respectively) with or without added milk over a 24 h period. A total urine collection was taken for the initial 6 h followed by a further 18 h. The oxalate content of the urine voided was measured using an enzyme kit method and the availability of the soluble oxalate consumed was measured for the 6 h and the total 24 h sample. The mean availability of the oxalate extracted from tea measured over a 6 h period ranged from 1.9 to 4.7 per cent when tea was consumed without milk and it was –3.0 to 2.3 per cent over 24 h period. These studies show that consuming black tea on a daily basis will lead to a moderate intake of soluble oxalate each day, but consumption of tea with milk on a regular basis would result in the absorption of very little oxalate from tea[54]. However, some studies have suggested tea consumption may affect the absorption of oxalates and contribute to the development of kidney stone[55]. In an examination of the prospective Nurses' Health Study, a cohort of more than 81,000 women of 40 to 65 years age, Curhan and coworkers found inverse association between tea consumption and the risk of kidney stone formation[56]. Employing a multivariate model that adjusted simultaneously for 17 beverages and other potential risk factors, for each 240 ml serving of tea consumed daily the risk of developing kidney stones appeared to be lowered by 8 per cent (CI: 1–15 per cent). An earlier study of 45,289 men reported a similar relationship with a 14 per cent decereased risk of developing kidney stones after tea consumption[57].

Diabetes

Some limited evidence from animal studies suggests that tea may have an effect on glucose tolerance in diabetes.[58] A study was conducted recently at the Shiseikai Daini hospital in Japan on the effects of various drinks on development of diabetes and it was observed that the group which drank green tea had fewer complications of diabetic nephropathy[59]. The prevention of the progress of diabetic nephropathy by consuming green and black tea in human and animal studies has also been reported[60, 61]. Tea suppresses the activity of glucose transporters in the intestinal epithelium and is believed to reduce dietary glucose intake[62]. A reduction in oxidative damage to lymphocyte DNA has been observed in diabetic patients receiving quercetin and tea.[63] In India, black tea extracts were found to possess preventive as well as curative effect on streptozotocin-induced diabetes in rats[64]. The active components of tea for blood glucose depressing activity are EGCG, TF digallate, TR, diphenylamine and polysaccharides. And the mechanism of inhibition of blood glucose level and the curing effect of tea on diabetes are: (1) inhibition of a-amylase and sucrose in intestine, thereby deterring the ingestion of certain amounts of sucrose or maltose; (2) inhibition of glucose absorption partially, thus leading to a reduction in blood glucose level; (3) inhibition of glycated albumin including fluorescent advanced glycolysation end products; and (4) free radical scavenging activity in the early stage of Maillard reaction (amino–carbonyl reaction)[65].

Anti-obesity Effects

Obesity has increased at an alarming rate in recent years and it is now a worldwide health problem. Disequilibrium between energy intake and expenditure is the probable cause of obesity. Obesity is known to be a strong risk factor for type 2 diabetes associated with insulin resistance. The stimulation of hepatic lipid metabolism might be a factor responsible for the anti-obesity effects of tea catechins. It has been reported that long-term consumption of tea catechins in C57BL/6J mice is beneficial for the suppression of diet-induced obesity, and it may reduce the risk of associated diseases including diabetes and coronary heart disease[66]. It was also confirmed that the dose of tea catechins (0.1–0.2 per cent) used in this study did not increase the fecal excretion of lipids. Dulloo and coworkers showed that ingestion of tea catechins stimulated O_2 consumption and energy expenditure and decreased the respiratory quotient in humans[67]. Further, it was recently demonstrated that long-term intake of tea catechins at 600 mg/day decreased visceral fat mass, as determined by computed tomography in humans[68]. Assuming that an infusion of green tea contains 1 g/1 catechins[69], daily intakes of 600 ml of green tea is expected to reduce body weight similarly[66]. Green tea extract thus seems to have the potential to influence body weight, although controlled trials on weight loss in humans are needed to further explore these preliminary observations.

In Japan, anti-obesity effect of oolong tea was reported in high-fat diet-treated mice and caffeine was found to enhance nonadrenaline induced lipolysis through acting of lipid droplets. The pancreatic lipase activity was also seen to be inhibited by the tea extract.[70] The effect may have broader implication because obesity increases the risks for cancer and CVD. It is also reported that green tea and caffeine have thermogenic properties, promote fat oxidation and play a role in the control of body composition probably via sympathetic activation of thermogenesis that can reduce obesity (Table 7.1). Caffeine and oolong teas can enhance nonadrenaline-induced lipolysis in fat cells, preventing obesity and fatty liver, and inhibit pancreatic lipase activity in obese mice induced by a high-fat diet[70]. In China, Rumpler and coworkers measured the impact of oolong tea on energy expenditure (EE) of humans [72]. They have reported that EE was significantly increased by 2.9 per cent and 3.4 per cent for the full strength tea (daily allotment brewed from 15 g of tea) and caffeinated water treatment (water containing 270 mg caffeine) respectively. Fat oxidation was reported to be significantly higher (12 per cent) when subjects consumed full strength tea rather than water. Recently, Kajimoto and coworkers investigated[72a] the effectiveness of 12 week consumption of a tea catechin-containing drink with little caffeine on body fat reduction and evaluated its safety in healthy adult men and women showing 22.5< body mass index $\leq$ 30 kg m^2. This study demonstrated that a drink containing tea catechins was effective in reducing body fat and safe when consumed continuously for 12 weeks. Although these effects were milder than those of medicines, it is useful because of its safety and availability for long-term intake. Therefore, tea catechin-containing drink may be beneficial for many people in whom moderate or mild overweight may increase the risk of lifestyle related disorders such as diabetes and hyperlipidemia.

Table 7.1

Effect of oral administration of caffeinated beverages on the thickness of the dermal fat layer under tumours of different sizes in SKH–1 mice previously treated with UV (high–risk mice)

	Thickness of dermal fat layer under tumours (μm)			
Tumour diameter (mm)	*Non-caffeinated plus caffeinated beverages*[a]	*Non-caffeinated beverages*[b]	*Caffeinated beverages*[b]	*Per cent decrease*
≤ 0.5	58 ± 3 (202)	70 ± 4 (100)	45 ± 2 (102)	36
0.5-1	49 ± 3 (204)	63 ± 3 (125)	27 ± 2 (79)	57
1-2	43 ± 3 (177)	54 ± 3 (125)	16 ± 2 (52)	70
2-3	31 ± 5 (56)	39 ± 5 (42)	4 ± 1 (14)	90
>3	24 ± 5 (50)	34 ± 6 (35)	1 ± 1 (15)	97
Mean Value	47 ± 1 (689)	58 ± 2 (427)	29 ± 2 (262)	50

UV-pretreated high-risk SKH-1 mice were treated orally with non-caffeinated beverages (water, dGT, dBT) or caffeinated beverages (GT, BT, CF, dGT+CF, and dBT+CF) (GT, green tea; BT, black tea; dGT, decaffeinated green tea; dBT, decaffeinated black tea; CF, caffeine) for 23 weeks. The thickness of the dermal fat layer under tumours of different sizes was measured in all 152 tumour-bearing mice (67 mice from the non- caffeinated beverage groups and 85 mice from the caffeinated beverage groups). The values in parentheses indicate the number of tumours studied. The mean value for the thickness of the dermal fat layer under tumours ±Se is given for tumours of different sizes.

[a] There was a significant negative linear association between tumour diameter and the log thickness of the dermal fat layer under tumours (P = 0.0001) using the random coefficient (hierarchical linear) model.

[b] The rate of decrease in thickness of the dermal fat layer under tumours of increasing size in mice treated with caffeinated beverages was significantly greater than that for mice treated with the non-caffeinated beverages (p = 0.0001) using the random coefficient (hierarchical linear) model.

Source: Ref. 71

Anti-arthritis Effects

Green tea polyphenols produce a significant reduction in arthritis incidence with a marked reduction of inflammatory mediators, of neutral endopeptidase activity, of IgG and type II collagen-specific IgG levels in arthritic joints in mice[73]. It was reported in a landmark study[74] that mice drinking green tea developed lower incidence and milder form of collagen-induced arthritis, which was similar to that of the arthritis of humans. Importantly, the biological markers of arthritis progression were found negatively regulated in the animals consuming green tea. In another prospective cohort study[75], comprising 31,336 women ages 55 to 69 years without a history of rheumatoid arthritis (RA), it was observed that women consuming $\geq$ 3 cups/day of tea displayed a decreased risk of RA compared with women who never drank tea. Multivariable adjustment for a number of potential confounders did not alter the result. It can be stated that the antioxidant present in tea might retard onset and incidence of arthritis.

Is Tea a Good Source of Minerals?

While potassium makes up the majority of the mineral content of tea, its score of less than 5 per cent of reference nutrient intake (RNI) derived from tea 'is no basis for any claim or significant statement'. Manganese is also present (see table 4.2), but as science has yet to find a proven health benefit from manganese ingested from tea and no RNI has been established, this doesn't work either, neither does aluminium (Al), which tea is actually high in. Tea is a major source of dietary Al intake. It is fairly *well established that drinking tea leads to measurable, but moderate increases in urinary Al excretion. The reported concentrations of Al in tea infusions are remarkably consistent and with few exceptions, values are in the range of 1–6 mg l^{-1}. However, the Al present in tea does not seem to be much more bioavailable than that from other dietary sources. Many consumers equate Al to Alzheimer's disease. However, researchers have consistently suggested that there is little or no scientific evidence to suggest that Al in tea poses any risk to human health.*

Tea provides 70 per plus of our daily fluoride intake. Fluoride from the soil accumulates naturally in the tea plant, but this is a double-edged sword: on one hand, fluoride has been shown to have a role in helping bones and teeth glow and to prevent diseases such as dental caries; on the other, too much fluoride has been associated with enhanced rates of bone cancer and skeletal and dental fluorosis. But do not fear, even if anybody drinks four to five cups of tea made with fluoridated water every day, he or she still would be ingesting amounts of fluoride well below the level of concern.

So overall, fairly tenuous evidences for pro-health enthusiasts, but reassuring for those concerned with possible effects of aluminium and fluoride.

Source: Ref. 84 & 85

Box 7.1

Antidiarrhoeal Effects

The effect of hot water extract of black tea (BTE) on upper gastrointestinal tract and on diarrhoea was investigated [76] in rodent models. BTE was found to possess antidiarrhoeal activity and indicated a role of the opioid system in the antidiarrhoeal activity of the BTE. Further, investigations are needed to verify these findings and explore their biological basis.

Antiallergic Effects

Progress in the management of allergic diseases including asthma, pollen diseases and atopic dermatitis has recently improved patients' quality of life. In addition to steroids, which are powerful inhibitors of allergic inflammation, other antiallergic compounds, humanised anti–IgE (immunoglobulin E) antibody and cytokine modulators have been developed. However, the worldwide prevalence of allergic diseases has increased during the last two decades, making early intervention to prevent the development of such diseases essential. Through analysis of the clinical evaluation of one kind of traditional remedy in patients with atopic dermatitis, flavonoids were shown to possess significant anti-allergic activity. They inhibited not only the release of chemical mediators but also the production of T–helper (Th)–2 type cytokines (Interleukin (IL)–4, IL–5 and IL–13) by basophils. Flavonoids inhibit expression of these cytokines through their inhibitory effect on the activation of several calcium-calmodulin dependent kinases. [77] In Japan, Fuzimura and coworkers observed that the *O*–methylated derivative of (–)-epigallocatechin–3–*0*–gallate (EGCG), (–)-epigallocatechin–3–*0*–(3–*0*–methyl)-gallate

(EGCG 3Me), which was isolated from tea leaves, could inhibit type 1 allergy more potently than EGCG[78]. They also suggested that EGCG 3Me could negatively regulate basophil activation through the suppression of Fc.Rl expression. It was also found that EGCG 3Me could inhibit histamine release in the human basophilic cell line KU812[79].

Skin and Eye Protection

Skin tissue is metabolically very active and highly susceptible to oxidative stress from environment and endogenous sources[10]. Chronic exposures to solar ultraviolet (UV) light of human skin results in photoaging. Green tea polyphenol (GTP) treatments have been found to inhibit UVB- induced protein oxidation *in vivo* in mouse skin, a hallmark of photoaging, by immunoblotting, and immunohistochemistry. Green tea polyphenol treatment has also been reported to inhibit UVB– induced protein oxidation *in vitro* in human skin fibroblast HS68 cells, which supports *in vivo* observations.[80] Further, oral administration of GTP also results in inhibition of UVB-induced expression of matrix degrading matrix metalloproteinases (MMP) such as MMP–2 (67 per cent), MMP–3 (63 per cent), MMP–7 (62 per cent), and MMP–9 (60 per cent) in hairless mouse skin. Black tea polyphenols also protect against UVB–induced erythema, tyrosine phosphorylation and inflammation response in mouse and human skin, and pretreatment can reverse the UVB–induced expression of early response genes[81, 82]. EGCG and ECG inhibit 5∝-reductase present in the skin and associated with androgen–dependent dermatologic disorders such as acne[83].

However, these data suggest that tea polyphenols as a dietary supplement could be useful to attenuate solar UVB light–induced premature skin aging and some dermatologic disorders.

EGCG can protect the rabbit eye lens against photooxidative stress induced by UVA. EGCG inactivated catalase induced by UVA exposure[84].

Iron Absorption

Iron deficiency is a major world health problem, that is, to a great extent, caused by poor iron absorption from the diet[87]. Tea, like other flavonoids—and phenolic—rich vegetables and fruits can inhibit the absorption of non-haem iron by the formation of insoluble complexes[88, 89], making the iron unavailable for absorption. However, this does not necessarily mean that high tea consumption is associated with an unfavourable iron status at the population level.[90] The bioavailability of non-haem iron appears to be inhibited by 79 per cent to 94 per cent when both are consumed concomitantly[91]. The impact of this interaction will be dependent on the iron intake and status of the individual. Iron deficiency anemia among children in UK[92] and the Saudi Arabia[93] may be exacerbated by the regular consumption of tea with meals. This effect, on the other hand, may be benefited for the patients with genetic hemochromatosis, as significant reduction in iron absorption was observed when 18 hemochromatosis patients included with their meals a tannin-rich tea instead of water[94]. The catechins of green tea may also have an affinity for iron. Samman and colleagues found 25 per cent reduction ($P < 0.05$) of non-haem iron absorption when they added 0.1 mmoles green tea extract to a single meal consumed by 27 women of 19 to 39 years age[95]. However, the general conclusion on the inhibitory effect of tea and iron absorption in humans can be formulated as: consumption of tea between meals inhibits the absorption of non-haem iron by 15–20 per cent whereas simultaneous consumption of black tea and iron-containing foods inhibits iron absorption by about 60–70 per cent, independently of the strength of the tea[87–89]. Negative effect of tea could be overcome by the presence of ascorbic acid containing orange juice or consuming tea between meals. Recently, Nelson and Poulter evaluated the literature on the likely impact of tea drinking on the iron status of different groups within the UK population and concluded[96] that there is no need to advise any restriction on tea drinking in healthy people with no risk of iron deficiency. In groups at risk of iron deficiency, people should drink tea between meals and to wait at least 1 h after eating before drinking tea.

Tea and Alzheimer's Disease

The functioning of the brain cholinergic system, which is involved in attention and memory, declines during normal ageing and is further affected in Alzheimer's disease[97]. In Alzheimers's disease and related disorders, viz. vascular dementia and dementia with Lewy bodies, there is a decline in cholinergic activity in the key areas involved in memory and cognition[98]. Current drugs for the symptomatic treatment of dementia are aimed at enhancing the associated cholinergic deficit by inhibiting acetylcholinesterase[99]. This is an enzyme which cleaves the neurotransmitter acetylcholine. Inhibiting the activities of cholinesterases (acetylcholinesterase and butyrylcholinesterase) should be one of the objectives in the treatment of cognitive dysfunctions associated with Alzheimer's disease[100]. It has been reported that green and black tea infusions *in vitro* inhibited human acetylcholinesterase and human butyrylcholinesterase[100] However, clinical and scientific investigation of the chemistry and activities of cholinomimetic and anti-β-secretase compounds in *Camellia sinensis* and cognitive effects of tea consumption is needed in order to establish the relevance of these findings.

Tea's Health Message and the Promotional Opportunities

Tea has always come with a positive health message ever since the Chinese started drinking it. The monk Eisai, considered the 'Father of Tea' in Japan, wrote in his book 'Maintaining Health by Drinking Tea' in 1211: 'Tea is a miraculous medicine for the maintenance of health. Tea has an extraordinary power to prolong life'. But in those days the health claims could not be substantiated by scientific evidence. Today, there is reliable body of scientific evidence that proves tea's positive health benefits. Although more comprehensive, in-depth cohort studies are needed to thoroughly evaluate the association between tea drinking and risk of chronic diseases, clinical research till date has revealed several physiological responses to tea which seem to be very relevant to the promotion of health. Ongoing research into the properties and possible benefits of tea are of tremendous importance to the industry as it struggles to promote tea over other the veracity of the various health claims espoused for tea. However, there is a general feeling that tea industry need to be very careful in what and how they say in communicating the health message direct to the customer. The outright claims are prohibited by law in some countries like USA. However, as an opportunity for brand promotions, the health story is undoubtedly a powerful one but the following basic guidelines should be kept in mind.

• Stick with the truth. • Keep it simple. • Know market intimately. • Devise ideas and images that use the scientific information in a way that speaks intelligently to the target audience.

Above all, tea is a great drink for modern lives: regardless of how it drinks, green, black with milk, lemon, sugar or spice—it is still a best bet.

Box 7.2

References

1. Goto, K, Kanaya, S, Nishikawa, T, Hara, H, Terada, A, Ishigami, T and Hara, Y (1998). The influence of tea catechins on fecal flora of elderly residents in long-term care facility. *Ann. Long-Term Care* **2**: 1–6.
2. Goto, K, Kanaya, S., Ishigami, T. and Hara, Y (1999). The effects of tea catechins on fecal conditions of elderly residents in a long-term care facility. *J. Nutr. Sci. Vitaminol.* **45**: 135-141.
3. Hara, Y (2001). *Green Tea: Health Benefits and Applications.* Marcel Dekker Inc, New York, p. 252.
4. Diker, K. S. and Hascelik, G (1994). The bacterial activity of tea against *Helicobacter pylori. Lett. Appl. .Microbiol.* **19**: 299–300.
5. Yang, CS, Kim, S, Yang, G-Y, Lee, M–J, Liao, J, Chung, JY and Ho, C–T (1999). Inhibition of carcinogenesis by tea:

bioavailability of tea polyphenols and mechanisms of actions. *Proc. Soc. Exp. Biol. Med.* **220**: 213-217.

6. Yamamoto, T, Juneja, LR, Chu, D–C. and Kim, M (1997). Chemistry and applications of green tea. CRC Press LLC: Boca Raton, USA.
7. Maity, S, Vedasiromoni, DR and Ganguly, DK (1998). Role of glutathione in the antiulcer effect of hot water extract of black tea (*Camellia sinensis*). *Jap. J. Pharmacol.* **78**: 285–292.
8. Toda, M, Okubo, S, Ikigai, H, Suzuki, T, Suzuki, Y and Shimamura, T (1991). The protective activity of tea against infection by Vibrio cholerae. *J. Appl. Bacteriol.* **70**: 109–112.
9. Diker, KS, Akan, M, Hascelik, G and Yurdakök, M. The bacterial activity of tea against *Campilobacter jejuni*, and *Campilobacter coli*. *Lett. Appl. Microbiol.* **12**: 34–35.
10. Dufresne, CJ and Farnworth, ER (2001). A review of latest research findings on the health promotion properties of tea. *J. Nutrl. Biochem.* **12**: 404–421.
11. Toda, M, Okubo, S, Hiyoshi, R and Tadakatsu, S (1989). The bactericidal activity of tea and Coffee. *Lett. Appl. Microbiol.* **8**:123–125.
12. Hamilton-Miller, JMT and Shah, S (1999). Disorganisation of cell division of methicillin-resistant *Staphylococcus aureus* by a component of tea (*Camellia sinensis*): a study by electron microscopy. *FEMS Microbiol. Lett.* **176**: 463–469.
13. Ghosal, S., Krishna Prasad, BN, Raj, K and Bhaduri, A.P (1993). Antiamoebic and antibacterial properties of black tea. *Proc. Intl. Symp. TEATECH, Tea Science and Human Health,* Jan. 11–14, 1993, Tea Research Association, Calcutta, 119–124.
14. Shantha, T, Rati, ER and Joseph, R (1996). Reversal of growth inhibition of *Bacillus megaterium* due to aflatoxin by coffee and tea extracts. *Lett. Appl. Microbiol.* **23**: 437–438.
15. Sugita, KY, Hara, KY, Amano, F, Okubo, T, Aoi, N, Iwaki, M and Kumagai, S (1999). Epigallocatechin gallate and gallocatechin gallate in green tea catechins inhibit extracellular release of Vero toxin from enterohemorragic *Escherichia coli* 0157:H7. *Bichem. Biophys. Acta.* **1472**: 42–50.

16. Sasaki, H, Matsumoto, M, Tanaka, T, Maeda, M, Nakai, M, Hamada, S and Ooshima, T (2004). Antibacterial activity of polyphenol components in Oolong tea extract against Streptococcus mutants. *Caries Res.* **38**: 2–8.
17. Takeo, T (2002). Exhilarating extract. *Contemporary Tea Time* 11: 7–9.
18. Kawai, KN, Tsuno, N, Kitayama, J, Okaji, Y, Yazawa, K, Asakage, M, Hori, N, Watanabe, T, Takahashi, K and Nagawa, H (2003). Epigallocatechin gallate, the main component of tea polyphenol, binds to CD4 and interferes with gp120 binding. *J. Allergy Clin. Immunol.* **112**: 951–957.
19. Nakane, H and Ono, K (1989). Differential inhibition of HIV-reverse transcriptase and various DNA and RNA polymerases by some catechin derivatives. *Nucleic Acids Research* **21**:115–116.
20. Fassina, G, Buffa, A, Benelli, R, Varnier, OE, Noonan, DM and Albini, A (2002). Polyphenolic antioxidant (–)-epigallocatechin–3–gallate from green tea as a candidate anti–HIV agent. *AIDS* **16**: 939–941.
21. Yamaguchi, K, Honda, M, Ikigai, H, Hara, Y and Shimamura, T (2002). Inhibitory effects of (–)–epigallocatechin gallate on the life cycle of human immunodeficiency virus type 1 (HIV–1). *Antiviral Res.* **53**: 19–34.
22. Nance, CL and Shearer, WT (2003). Is green tea good for HIV–1 infection? *J. Allergy Clin. Immunol.* **112**: 851–853.
23. McCormick, TG, Nance, Cl, Williamson, MP and Shearer, WT (2004). Green tea polyphenol epigallocatechin gallate binding to CD4 as a model for the inhibition of HIV–1–gp120 binding to CD4+T cells *J. Allergy. Clin. Immunol.* **113**: S256.
24. Weber, JM, Ruzindana-Umunyana, A., Imbeault, L and Sircar, S (2003). Inhibition of adenovirus infection and adenain by green tea catechin. *Antiviral Res.* **58**: 167–173.
25. Kamath, AB, Wang, L, Das, H, Li, L, Reinhold, VN and Bukowski, JF 2003. Antigens in tea beverage prime human gamma delta T cells in vitro and in vivo for memory and nonmemory antibacterial cytokine responses. *Proc. Natl. Acad. Sci.* **100**: 6009–6014.

26. Hamilton-Miller, JMT (2001). Anti-cariogenic properties of tea (*Camellia sinensis*). *J. Med. Microbiol.* **50**: 299–302.
27. Jones, C, Woods, K, Whittle, G, Worthington, H and Taylor, G (1999). Sugar, drinks, deprivation and dental caries in 14–year–old children in the north west of England in 1995. *Community Dent. Health* **16**: 68–71.
28. Rasheed, A and Haider, M (1998). Antibacterial activity of *Camellia sinensis* extracts against dental caries. *Arch. Pharm. Res.* **21**: 348–352.
29. Sarkar, S, Sett, P, Chowdhury, T and Ganguly, DK (2000). Effect of black tea on teeth. *J. Indian Soc. Pedod. Prev. Dent.* **18**: 139–140.
30. Sakanaka, S, Aizawa, M, Kim, M and Yamamoto, T (1996). Inhibitory effects of green tea polyphenols on growth and cellular adherence of an oral bacterium, *Porphyromonas gingivalis*. *Biosci. Biotech. Biochem.* **60**: 745–749.
31. Kakuda, T, Takihara, T, Sakane, I and Mortelmans, K (1994). Antimicrobial activity of tea extracts against peridontopathic bacteria. *Nippon Nogeikagaku Kaishi* **68**: 241–243.
32. Simpson, A, Shaw, L and Smith, AJ (2001). Tooth surface pH during drinking of black tea. *Br. Dent. J.* **190: 374–376.**
33. Zhu, M, Wei, G and Wu, C (2003). Effect of tea polyphenols on growth and H_2S production of halitosis causing bacteria. *103rd General Meeting of the American Soc. Microbiol.* Washington, DC, May 18–22, 2003.
34. Schiffenbauer, M, Garden, I, Moscato, M, Savides, N and Yastrovskaya, D (2003). The antimicrobial effect of green tea and polyphenol. *103rd General Meeting of the American Soc. Microbiol.* Washington, DC, May 18–22, 2003.
35. Schiffenbauer, M, Gandhi, J, George, G, Goldshteyn, A, Livshits, E and Welsh, N (2004). The antimicrobial effect of green tea and polyphenol. *104 th General Meeting of the American Soc. Microbiol.* New Orleans, LA., May 23–27, 2003.
36. Kavanagh, D and Renehan, (1998). Fluoride in tea- its dental significance: a review. *J. Ir. Dent. Assoc.* **44**: 100-105
37. Simpson, A, Shaw, L and Smith, AJ (2001). The bioavailability of fluoride from black tea. *J. Dentistry* **29**: 15–21.

38. Zhang, J and Kashker, S (1998). Inhibition of salivary amylase by black and green teas and their effects on the intraoral hydrolysis of starch. *Caries Res.* **32**: 233-238.
39. Lizuka, S 1980. Inhibitory effect of tannic acid on the lactate metabolism in human saliva. *Dentistry* **67**: 770–778.
40. Itoh, T (1991). Inhibition of cariogenic factor of mutants streptococci by tannic acid. *Nihon Univ. J. Oral. Sci.* **17**: 115–126.
41. Wu-Yuah, CD, Chen, CY and Wu, RT (1988). Gallotannins inhibit growth, water insoluble glucan synthesis and aggregation of mutants Streptococci. *J. Dent. Res.* **67**: 51–55.
42. Yu, H, Oho, T and Xu, LX (1995). Effects of several tea components on acid resistance of human tooth enamel. *J. Dentistry* **23**: 101–105.
43. Cummings, SR, Kelsey, JL, Nevitt, MC and O'Dowd, KJ (1985). Epidemiology of osteoporosis and osteoporotic fractures. *Epidemiol. Rev.* **7**: 178–208.
44. Santora, AC (1987). Role of nutrition and exercise in osteoporosis. *Am. J. Med.* **82**: 73–79.
45. Hegarty, VM, May, HM and Khaw, Kay–Tee (2000). Tea drinking and bone mineral density in older women. *Am. J. Clin. Nutr.* **71** : 1003–1007.
46. Johnell, O, Gullberg, B, Kanis, JA, Allander, E, Elffors, L, Dequeker, J, Dilsen, G, Gennari, C, Lopes Vaz, A, Lyritis, G (1995). Risk factors for hip fracture in European women: the MEDOS study. Mediterranean Osteoporosis Study. *J. Bone Miner. Res.* **10**: 1802-1815.
47. Kanis, J, Johnell, O, Gulberg, B (1999). Risk factors for hip fracture in men from southern Europe: the MEDOS study. Mediterranean Osteoporosis Study. *Osteoporos Ins.* **9**: 45–54.
48. Hoover, PA, Webber, CE, Beaumont, LF, and Blake, JM (1996). Postmenopausal bone mineral density: relationship between calcium intake, calcium absorption, residual estrogen, body composition and physical activity. *Can. J. Physiol. Pharmacol.* **74**: 911–917.
49. Hernandez-Avilla, M, Stampfer, MJ and Ravnikar, VA (1993). Caffeine and other predictors of bone density

among pre– and perimenopausal women. *Epidemiology* **4**: 128–134.

50. Wu, C–H, Yang, Y–C, Yao, W–J, Lu, F–H, Wu, J–S and Chang, C–J (2002). Epidemiological evidence of increased bone mineral density in habitual tea drinkers. *Arch. Intern. Med.* **162**: 1001–1006.
51. Chen, Z, Pettinger, MB, Ritenbaugh, C, LaCroix, AZ, Robbins, J, Caan, BJ, Barad, DH and Hakim, IA (2003). Habitual tea consumption and risk of osteoporosis: a prospective study in the women's health initiative observational cohort. *Am. J. Epidemiol.* **158**: 772–781.
52. Krall, EA, and Dawson-Hughes, B (1999). Osteoporosis. In: *Nutrition in Health and Disease*, 9 th ed., (ed.), Shils M Williams & Wilkins, Baltimore, pp. 1353–1364.
53. Basu, S, Michaelsson, K, Olofsson, H, Johansson, S and Melhus, H (2001). Association between oxidative stress and bone mineral density. *Biochem. Biophys. Res. Commun.* **288**: 275–279.
54. Savage, GP, Charrier, MJS and Vanhanen, L (2003). Bioavailability of soluble oxalate from tea and the effect of consuming milk with the tea. *Eur. J. Clin. Nutr.* **57**: 415–419.
55. Massey, L Tea oxalate. (2000). *Nutr. Rev.* **58**: 89-89.
56. Curhan, GC, Willett, WC, Speizer, F, and Stampfer, MJ (1998). Beverage use and risk of kidney stones in women. *Ann. Intern. Med.* **128**: 534–540.
57. Curhan, GC, Willett, WC, Rimm, EB, Spiegelman, D and Stampfer, MJ (1996). Progressive study of beverage use and the risk of kidney stones. *Am. J. Epidemiol.* **143**: 240–247.
58. Jhawar, RS (2000). *Tea—the Universal Health Drink.* UBS Publisher's Distributors Ltd., New Delhi, p 89, p 59.
59. Yoshihara, Y, Honda, M, Takano, Y and Mogi, M (2001). Intake of green tea of a diabetic. *Proc. Intl. Conf. O-Cha (tea) Culture and Science*, Session III, Oct 5–8, 2001, Shizuoka, Japan, 226–229.
60. Takano, Y, Honda, M, Yoshihara, Y (2001). The effect of drinking green tea on diabetic nephropathy. *Proc. Intl. Conf. O–Cha (tea) Culture and Science*, Session III, Oct. 5-8, 2001, Shizuoka, Japan, 218–221.

61. Vinson, JA, Wu, N, Teufel, K and Zhang, J (2001). Beneficial effects of green and black tea on animal models of atherosclerosis and diabetes. *Proc. Intl. Conf. O-Cha (tea) Culture and Science*, Session III, Oct 5–8, 2001, Shizuoka, Japan, 367.
62. Shimizu, M (1999). Modulation of the intestinal function by food substances. *Nahrung* **43**: 154–158.
63. Lean, ME, Norozi, M, Kelly, I., Burns, J, Talwar, D, Sattar, N and Crozier, A (1999). Dietary flavonols protect diabetic humans lymphocytes against oxidative damage to DNA. *Diabetes* **48**: 176–181.
64. Gomes, A, Vedasiromoni, JR, Das, M, Sharma, RM and Ganguly, DK (1995). Antihyperglycemic effect of black tea (*Camellia sinensis*) in rat. *J. Ethnopharmacol.* **45**: 2223–2226.
65. Chen, Z 2003. Pharmacological functions of tea. *Planters' Chronicle* **99**: 20–37.
66. Murase, T, Nagasawa, A, Suzuki, J, Hase, T and Tokimitsu, I (2002). Beneficial effects of tea catechins on diet-induced obesity: stimulation of lipid catabolism in the liver *Intl. J. Obesity* **26**: 1459-1464.
67. Dulloo, AG, Duret, C, Rohrer D, Girardier, L, Mensi, N, Fathi, M, Chantre, P and Vandermander, J (1999). Efficacy of a green tea extract rich in catechin polyphenols and caffeine in increasing 24-h energy expenditure and fat oxidation in humans. *Am. J.* Clin. Nutr. ***70**: 1040–5.*
68. Nagao, T, Meguro, S, Soga, S, Otsuka, A, Tomonobu, K, Fumoto, S, Chikama, A., Mori, K, Yuzawa, M, Watanabe, H, Hase, T, Tanaka, Y, Tokimitsu, I., Shimasaki, H and Itakura, H (2001). Tea catechins suppress accumulation of body fat in humans. *J. Oleo. Sci.* **50**: 717–728.
69. Scalbert, A. and Williamson, G 2000. Dietary intake and bioavailability of polyphenols. *J. Nutr.* **130**: 2073S–2085S.
70. Han, L–K, Takaku, T, Li, J, Kimura, Y and Okuda, H (1999). Anti-obesity action of oolong tea. *Obesity* **23**: 98–105.
71. Conney, AH, Lu, Y–P, Lou, Y–R. and Huang, M–T (2002). Inhibitory effects of tea and caffeine on UV-induced carcinogenesis: relationship to enhanced apoptosis and decreased tissue fat. *Eur. J. Cancer. Prev.* **11** (suppl 2): S28–S36.

72. Rumpler, W, Seale, J, Clevidence, B, Judd, J, Wiley, E, Yamamoto, S, Komatsu, T, Sawaki, T, Ishikura, Y and Hosoda, K (2001). Oolong tea increases metabolic rate and fat oxidation in men. *J. Nutr.* **131**: 2848–2852.

72a. Kajimoto, O, Kajimoto, Y, Yabune, M, Nakamura, T, Kotani, K, Suzuki, Y, Nozawa, A, Nagata, K, Unno, T, Sagesaka, YM, Kakuda, T and Yoshikawa, T (2005). Tea catechins with galloylmoiety reduce body weight and fat. *J. Health Sci.* **51**: 161-171.

73. Haqqi, TM, Anthony, DD, Gupta, S, Ahmad, N, Lee, MS, Kumar, GK and Mukhtar, H (1999). Prevention of collagen-induced arthritis in mice by a polyphenolic fraction from green tea. 1999. *Proc. Natl. Acad. Sci.* **96**: 4524–4529.

74. Mukhtar, H (2000). Tea in prevention of cancer, heart diseases, stroke and arthiritis. *Proc. Intl. Millennium Tea Convention*, Session 4, 22–24 March, 2000, New Delhi, India, 1–37.

75. Mikuls, TR, Cerhan, JR, Criswell, LA, Merlino, L, Mudano, A.S, Burma, M, Folsom, AR and Saag, KG (2002). Coffee, tea, and caffeine consumption and risk of rheumatoid arthritis: results from the Iowa women's health study. *Arthritis & Rheumatism* **46**: 83–91.

76. Besra, SE, Gomes, A., Ganguly, DK and Vedasiromoni, JR (2003). Antidiarrhoeal activity of hot water extract of black tea. *Phytotherapy Research* **17**: 380–384.

77. Tanaka, T, Higa, S, Hirano, T, Kotani, M, Matsumoto, M, Fujita, a and Kawasi, I (2003). Flavonoids as potential anti-allergic substances. *Current Medicinal Chem. Anti-inflammatory & Anti-allergy* **2**: 57–65.

78. Fujimura, Y, Tachibana, H, Yamamoto, MM Miyase, T, Sano, M and Yamada, K (2002). Antiallergic tea catechins, (–)–Epigallocatechin–3–*0*–(3–*0*–methyl)–gallate, suppresses F—RI expression in human basophilic KU812 cells. *J. Agric. Food Chem.* **50**: 5729–5734.

79. Tachibana, H, Sunada, Y, Miyase, T, Sano, M, Yamamoto-Maeda, M and Yamada, K (2000). Identification of a methylated tea catechins as inhibitor of degranulation in human basophilic KU812 cells. *Biosci. Biotechnol. Biochem.* **64**: 452–454.

80. Vayalil, PK, Mittal, A, Hara, Y, Elmets, CA and Katiyar, SK (2004). Green tea polyphenols prevent ultraviolet light-induced oxidative damage and matrix Metalloproteinases expression in mouse skin. *J. Investig. Dermatol.* **122**: 1480–1487.
81. Zhao, Z, Jin, XEY, Zheng, ZS, Zhang, YZ, Athar, M, DeLeo, VA, Mukhtar, H, Bickers, DR and Wang, ZY (1999). Photoprotective effect of black tea extracts against UVB-induced phototoxicity in skin. *Phytochem. Phytobiol.* **70**: 637–644.
82. Katiyar, S. K., Matsui, MS, Elmets, CA and Mukhtar, H (1999). Polyphenolic antioxidant (–)–epigallocatechin-3–gallate from green tea reduces UVB–induced inflammatory responses and infiltration of leucocytes in human skin. *Phytochem. Phytobiol.* **69**: 148–153.
83. Alex, AF, Jones, VA and Stiller, MJ (1999). Potential therapeutic applications of tea in dermatology. *Int. J. Dermatol.* **38**: 735–743.
84. Zigman, S, Rafferty, NS., Rafferty. KA and Lewis, N (1999). Effects of green tea polyphenols on lens photooxidative stress. *Biol. Bull.* **197**: 285–286.
85. Anonymous (2003). Tea & Health. *Tea & Coffee Asia* **5**: 27–29.
86. Flaten, TP (2002). Aluminium in tea—concentrations, speciationand bioavailability. *Coord. Chem. Rev.* **228**: 285–395.
87. Zijp, IM, Korver, O and Tijburg, BM (2000). Effect of tea and other dietary factors on iron absorption. *Critical Rev. Food Sci. Nutr.* **40**: 371–398.
88. Brune, M, Rossander, L and Hallberg, L (1989). Iron absorption and phenolic compounds: importance of different phenolic structures. *Eu. J. Clin. Nutr.* **43**: 547–558.
89. Reddy, MB, Hurrell, R and Cook, J (2000). Estimation of non-heme iron bioavailability from meal composition. *Am. J. Clin. Nutr.* **71**: 937–943.
90. Temme, EHM and Hoydonck, Van PGA (2002). Tea consumption and iron status. *Eu. J. Clin. Nutr.* **56**: 379-386.

91. Hurrell, RF, Reddy, M and Cook, JD (1999). Inhibition of non-haem iron absorption in man by polyphenolic-containing beverages. *Br. J. Nutr.* **81**: 289–295.
92. Gibson, S (1999). Iron intake and iron status of preschool children: associations with breakfast cereals, vitamin C and meat. *Public Health Nutr.* **2**: 521–528.
93. al-Othaimeen, A., Osman, A. and al Orf, S (1999). Prevalence of nutritional anaemia among primary school girls in Riyadh city, Saudi Arabia. *Int. J. Food Sci. Nutr.* **50**: 237–243.
94. Kaltwasser, J, Warner, E, Schalk, K, Hansen, C, Gottschalk, R and Seidl, C (1999). Clinical trial on the effect of regular tea drinking on iron accumulation in genetic haemochromatosis. *Gut* **43**: 699-704.
95. Samman, S, Sandstrom, Toft MB, Bukhave, K, Jensen, M, Sorensen, SS and Hansen, M (2001). Green tea or rosemary extract added to foods reduces non-heme iron absorption. *Am. J. Clin. Nutr.* **73**: 607–612.
96. Nelson M and Poulter, J (2004). Impact of tea drinking on iron status in the UK: a review. *J. Human Nutr. Dietetics* **17**: 43–59.
97. Perry, R, Watson, P and Hodges, JR, (2000). The nature and staging of attention dysfunction in early (minimal and mild) Alzheimer's disease: relationship to episodic and semantic memory impairment. *Neuropsychologia* **38**: 252–271.
98. Grantham, C and Geerts, H (2002). The rationale behind cholinergic drug treatment for dementia related to cerebrovascular disease. *J. Neurol. Sci.* **203–4**: 131–136.
99. Rosler, M, Anand, R, Cicin-Sain, A, Gauthier, S, Agid, Y, Dal-Bianco, P, Stähelin, HB, Hartman, R., Gharabawi, M. and Bayer, T (1999). Efficacy and safety of rivastigmine in patients with Alzheimer's disease: international randomized control trial. *Br. Med. J.* **318**: 633–638.
100. Okello, EJ, Savelev, SU and Perry, EK (2004). *In vitro* anti-â-secretase and dual anti-cholinesterase activities of *Camellia sinensis* L (tea) relevant to treatment of dementia. 2004. *Phytother. Res.* **18**: 624–627.

Glossary

AIDS

Acquired Immune Deficiency Syndrome, a disease that attacks the body's immune system, rendering it unable to fight diseases. AIDS is caused by a microorganism called the human immunodeficiency virus (HIV), transmitted by body fluids through sexual intercourse, the use of non sterile hypodermic needles, and contact with infected blood.

Alzheimer's Disease

A form of presenile dementia caused by atrophy of the prefrontal areas of the brain.

Amino Acid

Any of the group of organic compounds that form the basic constituents of protein.

Anaemia

A shortage of red blood cells or a deficiency of haemoglobin, the pigment in red blood cells that carries oxygen. Anaemia can result in a number of symptoms including weakness, tiredness and pale skin.

Antioxidants

Antioxidants are compounds that help to inhibit many oxidation reactions caused by free radicals thereby preventing or delaying damage to the cells and tissues. Their mechanisms of action include:

(i) scavenging of reactive oxygen species and reactive nitrogen species
(ii) chelating metal ions preventing, the generation of free radicals
(iii) decreasing the localised oxygen concentration thereby reducing molecular oxygen's oxidation potential
(iv) metabolising lipid peroxides to non-radical products.

Artery

A vascular tube that carries blood from the heart to the various tissues. The internal endothelial lining provides a smooth surface to prevent clotting of blood. The middle layer of plain muscle and elastic fibre allows for distension as blood is pumped from the heart. The outer, mainly connective tissues layer prevents over distension.

Arthritis

Any inflammation of the joints. Arthritis causes swelling, pain, and stiffness in the joints.

Asthma

An allergic condition marked by attacks of laboured breathing with wheezing and usually coughing, gasping, and a sense of constriction in the chest.

Atherosclerosis

A condition of the arteries in which blood flow is blocked by fatty deposits. This causes a thickening or 'furring' up of the lining of the artery walls, resulting in the narrowing of these arteries and increasing the risk of thrombosis. If this narrowing occurs in the coronary arteries it can result in angina and a blockage could result in a heart attack.

Atrophy

The degeneration or wasting away of an organ or part of the body, as from disease or disuse.

Basophil

A white blood cell with basophilic granules.

Bile

A bitter, alkaline, viscid, greenish-yellow fluid secreted by the liver and stored in the gall bladder.

Bladder

A membranous sac containing fluid or gas.

Blood

The red viscid fluid filling the heart and blood vessels, consisting of a colourless fluid, plasma, in which are suspended the red blood corpuscles (erythrocytes), white corpuscles (leucocytes), and the platelets (thrombocytes).

Blood pressure

Pressure exerted by blood on the walls of the blood vessels.

Blood serum

The fluid which exudes when blood clots.

Cancer

It is not a single disease, but rather a number of diseases characterised by uncontrolled growth and spread of abnormal cells in the body that are caused by both internal and external factors.

Capillaries

Extremely tiny blood vessels that connect the arteries and the veins.

Carcinogen

Any substance or agent that can promote the formation of a cancerous growth.

Carcinoma

Any of the malignant cancerous growths of the cells that line organs.

Chelating agents

Soluble organic substances that can fix metallic particles into their structure, often used to trap or remove heavy metal ions. In the case of free radicals, antioxidants can act as chelating agents preventing certain metallic ions from becoming free radicals.

Chemotherapy

Treatment of disease with the use of chemicals.

Cholesterol

A component of animal fat, blood, nerve tissue, and bile, some of which is necessary to a healthy body, but may be harmful in excess, as in the formation of atherosclerosis. As cholesterol is not soluble in the blood it is carried around by special proteins called lipoproteins, including:

(i) Low Density Lipoproteins (LDL) – high circulating levels are thought to be a risk factor for heart diseases
(ii) High Density Lipoproteins (HDL) – takes cholesterol away from the blood vessels and so high circulating levels are thought to be protective against heart diseases.

Collagen

The main protein constituent of white fibrous tissue.

Colon

The part of the large intestine that extends from the caecum to the rectum.

CTC

It stands for crush, tear and curl. CTC machine consists of two toothed rollers which move at different speeds in opposite directions. The leaf moves continuously between the rollers. CTC machine produces smaller pieces than the orthodox rollers.

Dental Caries

Progressive decay of the teeth.

Diabetes Insipidus

A disorder of the pituitary gland characterised by intense thirst and excretion of large amounts of urine.

Diabetes Mellitus

A disorder of the process by which the body uses sugars and other carbohydrates in which not enough insulin is produced by the body or the cells become resistant to its action. It is characterised typically by abnormally great amounts of sugar in the blood and urine.

Dietary Fibre

Coarse food containing much indigestible vegetable fibre composed mainly of cellulose.

Diuretic

An agent that promotes the excretion of urine.

DNA

Deoxyribonucleic Acid is the genetic material found in every cell of the body. The sequencing of this genetic material determines the unique properties and functions of cells. Damage to DNA, possibly due to a carcinogen, may result in the disturbance of the cell's control mechanisms, possibly resulting in cancer.

E. coli

One of a number of strains of rod-shaped bacteria that live in the intestinal tracts of humans and other animals.

Endothelium

Normal function of the inner lining of blood vessels, known as the endothelium, plays an important role in preventing cardiovascular diseases.

Epidemiological studies/Population studies

A type of observational study investigating health related states within populations. Whilst being useful for establishing theories about causes of diseases, they cannot establish a direct cause and effect relationship.

Fermentation/Oxidisation of tea leaves

The reaction that tea leaves undergo when they have been cut and exposed to air. The extent of oxidisation determines whether the final tea is green, oolong or black.

Flavonoids

Flavonoids are a subclass of the polyphenols, which are characterised as containing two or more aromatic rings, each bearing at least one aromatic hydroxyl and connected with a carbon bridge. They are found predominantly in tea, and have been associated with a wide range of biological activities, including antiangiogenic, antibacterial, anticarcinogenic, anti-inflammatory, antithrombobic, antiviral, hypocholesterolemic, hypoglycemic and vasodilatory effects.

Gastric cancer

A cancer of the digestive tract. It occurs most frequently in men over 40 years old. The incidence of gastric cancer is extremely high in Japan, Chile, and Iceland.

Gastritis

Inflammation of the stomach, especially the mucous membrane lining. Gastritis can result in severe blood loss and increased risk of gastric cancer if not treated.

Haemaglobin

The iron-containing, oxygen carrying molecule of the red blood cells of vertebrates comprising four polypeptic subunits in a heme group.

Hormone

A chemical messenger produced by endocrine glands and secreted directly into the blood stream to exert a specific effect on a distant part of the body.

Hypertension

Abnormally high blood pressure.

Inflammation

The reaction of living tissues to injury, infection or irritation; characterised by pain, redness, swelling and heat.

Insulin

A hormone produced by the islet cells of the pancreas that is responsible for the control of blood sugar levels.

***In-vitro* studies**

Tests or studies of biological processes or reactions that are made to occur outside the body in artificial conditions, often in a test tube.

***In-vivo* studies**

Studies where a biological process or reaction occurs or is carried out within a living tissue.

Ischemia

A deficiency of blood in an organ or part of the body. Ischemia is caused by obstruction of the blood vessels that supply an organ or area of the body. Such obstruction may be the result of narrowing, compression, or damage from conditions such as blood clot or atherosclerosis and causes oxygen loss that leads to tissue death in the affected area.

Kidney

Either of a pair of organs involved with the elimination of water and waste products from the body of vertebrates.

Leukaemia

A cancer of the blood forming organs, resulting in an abnormal increase in the number of leucocytes in the tissues of the body, with or without a corresponding increase of leucocytes circulating in the blood.

Lipids

Water insoluble fats that include cholesterol and triglycerides. They serve as a source of fuel, are an important constituent of cell membranes as well as have an important role in cardiovascular diseases.

Lipoprotein

Any of a number of compounds in the body such as those formed by the combination of cholesterol with fats and proteins. See cholesterol.

Menstrual cycle

The periodic series of changes associated with menstruation and the inter-menstrual cycle; menstrual bleeding indicates onset of the cycle.

Meta-analysis

A method that uses statistical techniques for combining results from different studies to obtain an estimate of the overall effect of a particular intervention. This combination may produce a stronger conclusion than can be provided by any individual study.

Metabolism

Chemical processes that occur in living organisms.

Metal ion

A metal that has either lost or gained an electron making it unstable. In an attempt to stabilise, it attacks other molecules which can lead to cell damage.

Nitrosamines

Molecules that are suspected carcinogens.

Nutrient

A substance serving as or providing nourishment.

Nutrition

The sum total of processes by which the living organism receives and utilises the minerals necessary for survival, growth and repair of worn-out tissues.

Obesity

The deposition of excess fat around the body, particularly in the subcutaneous tissue.

Observational study

A study in which the investigators observe large groups or individuals who are (and sometimes individuals who are not) exposed to the intervention over a period of time and interpret the outcomes. The investigators do not actively intervene in this type of study.

Orange pekoe

Referring to size of leaf, not quality or flavour, this term indicates a larger-size grade of whole leaf teas.

Orthodox

This is the traditional method of processing. Prepared using a technique which leads to larger leaf styles mirroring hand-produced teas.

Osteoporosis

Loss of bone density caused by excessive absorption of calcium and phosphorus from the bone, due to progressive loss of the protein matrix of bone which normally carries the calcium deposits.

Pan fired

Tea that is steamed and then agitated in an iron wok over a fire.

Parkinson's disease

A degenerative brain disorder that dramatically affects motor regions of the brain, leaving mental function completely intact. Characterised by symptoms such as body tremors, loss of facial expression, joint rigidity and slow movements in the limbs.

Pekoe

Whole leaf black tea produced by a medium plucking of the second leaf on the tea bush (The word Pekoe comes from the Chinese meaning 'white hair' and was originally applied to the early tea pluckings, due to the white down on the backs of the young leaf tea.)

pH

The standard measure of acidity. It is the negative logarithm of the hydrogen ion concentration. The neutral point is at a value of 7. Higher values are alkaline, lower are acidic.

Phytochemical

A group of chemicals arising from plants that include carotenoids, polyphenols and phytoestrogens.

Plasma

The fluid fraction of blood.

Platelet

Tiny blood cells involved in the clotting of blood; activated by tissue damage. Activation and aggregation of platelets is an important part in the development of atherosclerosis.

Platelet aggregation

Clumping of platelets together to repair injuries to a vessel wall. Over time this can contribute to atherosclerosis.

Polyphenols

Astringent compounds present in tea.

Prostate

A small conical gland at the base of the male bladder and surrounding the first part of the urethra.

Serum

Supernatant fluid which forms when blood clots.

Stroke

The sudden disruption of blood supply to an area of the brain; apoplexy.

Tannin

Erroneous term referring to the astringent polyphenols of tea, unrelated to tannic acid polyphenols of other plants.

Theaflavins

Orange red potyphenols unique to fermented teas such as black tea, and formed from the condensation of two catechins.

Theanine

Unique amino acid in tea.

Thrombosis

The intravascular formation of a blood clot.

Tumorigenesis

Development of a tumour.

Vascular endothelium

The inner lining of cells in all blood vessels that is known to play a central role in the regulation of blood vessel function.

Vasodilatation

A widening of the internal space within blood vessels.

Vitamin

Vitamin is an organic compound that cannot be manufactured in the cells of the body but needed in small quantities for operation of normal bodily metabolism. Vitamins in low concentrations have catalytic and regulatory functions in cell metabolism. A deficiency in the food of any vitamin produces deficiency symptoms. Overdoses of certain vitamins also have toxic effects.